How to Write a Business Plan with No Experience

A Simple Guide with Tons of Business Plan Examples to Achieve a Successful Business and Attain Profitability

Richard Hedberg

Table of Contents

Your Free Gift   v
Introduction   vii

1. Introduction to a Business Plan   1
2. How to Create a Business Plan   23
3. Building Relationships with Customers   64
4. Know Your Key Resources   82
5. Pitch Your Business Plan   95
6. Business Plans for Common Businesses   109
7. Business Planning Mistakes and How to
   Overcome Them   150

Conclusion   159
Thank You   161
References   163

Your Free Gift

As a way of saying thank you for your purchase, I'm offering the ebook, *Marketing on Click LLC: A Business Plan Example*, for FREE to my readers.

To get instant access, just go to:
https://prosperwithrichard.com/business-plan-free-bonus

Inside this ebook you will discover:

• Insider knowledge on formatting and structuring a winning business plan
• Proven strategies for what information to include and how to present it
• Secrets to using the right language and terminology to capture the attention of investors
• Exclusive insights on identifying potential gaps or weaknesses in your own plan
• The key to creating a business proposal that sets you apart from the competition
• And so much more!

Don't miss out on this opportunity to unlock the secrets of a winning business plan. Grab your free ebook today and start creating a plan that will take your business to the next level!

Introduction

Some people dream of success, while other people get up every morning and make it happen.

— Wayne Huizenga

Change isn't Difficult if You Know What You're Doing

Have you ever woken up in the morning feeling anxious about your day ahead? Is this a problem you are still experiencing? I used to be like you. Every morning, I would wake up with barely enough energy to get going. My 9-to-5 felt like a chore, and gradually my anxiety grew to the point where each day felt less and less like I was really living. I wasn't passionate about what I did because I felt I was being held back from expressing my talent. I didn't play a major role when I felt I should be achieving more. Additionally, my days became tiring, and this soon affected both my mental and physical health. I worked overtime on most days, and as a result, I barely had any time to spend with my family. I can still remember those days when I despised every minute. And all for what? Just to get that paycheck and miss out on every important moment in my family's life? Furthermore, I was missing out on what I wanted to do.

Fast forward a couple of years later, and I now wake up with full energy, looking forward to what my day will bring. I practice gratitude daily and always make plans using a journal first thing in the morning while I have breakfast with my family. I look forward to the things I've planned to do each day, and I now have enough flexibility to spend precious time with my family. I want to be there for my children during the most important days of their lives. I don't work a 9-to-5 anymore. I'm an entrepreneur who found success by nailing down the fundamentals of how a business should function, and now I'm living in California, living my life to the fullest with financial security.

This is the story of my transformation. Many of us assume correctly that change is pretty hard, and yes, it is hard, but it doesn't have to be overwhelming. I was able to make a trans-formation by owning many businesses and helping them thrive. Being an entrepreneur was my light at the end of the road to freedom, where I escaped the rat race a lot of us get trapped in. We are told as kids in schools to get a degree and work a 9-to-5 to gain a respectable status. Whenever someone did something outside the box, it was seen as an anomaly and eyebrows were raised. Due to these expectations, many avoid taking risks that could lead to a better life because they are afraid of failure or being judged by their peers for being different. Indeed, there are many other reasons that keep us from going outside our comfort zones. Having a successful business is one of them. You are putting in capital, and when things are done right, you achieve a profitable return on what you initially invested. This is what we call an ROI, or Rate on Investment. And this ROI can compound into millions.

Focus on the Opportunity, not the Resistance

Nowadays, there are many millionaires on this planet, and you may not believe it, but the average age of people reaching a millionaire status keeps going down each year. You have young adults in their early 20s becoming million-aires each year now. Most of them didn't need a degree or spend years gaining "industry exposure." They succeeded because they saw an opportunity and took advantage of it. The introduction of technology, or simply the digital age, has served as leverage; humans are usually at their peak form when they leverage the tools they've got at their disposal. Without tools, we can be powerless, but with tools, we are unstoppable. The digital era has presented numerous opportu-nities for anyone in the world to learn, plan, craft, and achieve a profitable business of any kind and know financial freedom. Times have changed, and we are now in an era where the market keeps changing while at the same time, the number of opportunities is increasing. You probably just haven't realized it yet.

I run many successful businesses because I've leveraged technology and the digital era and simply went for it. You have to take that risk in order to explore whether you are right or wrong about the whole thing. And you have every right to do this. I had the same feeling as you when I was starting out. I was pessimistic when I started exploring the idea of setting up my own business. First and foremost, I was worried about the financial requirements, and I was also afraid that I would waste most of my savings on something that would turn out to be a huge failure and waste of time. I was worried that I couldn't convince my wife and family about this risk I was going to take with all our finances, and I worried whether I would get any support. I was worried that if I didn't see any profits in the first few months, I would have to declare this venture a failure and walk the hall of shame.

Also, I was worried I would join the list of other entrepreneurs who have failed to run their business, as I was surrounded by people who were always telling stories about entrepreneurs who failed miserably in just months. Eventually, a lot of them end up going bankrupt. However, all my worries ended when I realized I'd been thinking from the wrong perspective. My way of thinking changed when I contemplated this question: Will my business solve a problem?

This May Change Your Opinion About Businesses

We've been thinking about businesses all wrong. We all think it will turn into a money-making machine after we put in some investment, like it will work its own magic. This is an incorrect way of thinking, but many people take it for granted. This mindset only leads us toward failure as entrepreneurs, but what if you changed your perspective—am I providing value to people and solving their problems? It is all about one thing, and that is value. Do you know if your business is changing people's lives in a positive way that you can see? This is what we call providing value to someone. In other words, you've developed a *value proposition*. A value proposition is simply an innovative feature or service that makes your product or business attractive in the eyes of your target market. For that, you will need to first identify the problem in the market. In this process, you identify a sector of people who have a particular problem and learn about their different pain points. Then, you craft a solution. You have found the problem, and now you are there to fix it. Find out how you can solve their problems and reverse-engineer everything from there. This is how an entrepreneur should develop his or her mindset, and this leads to attaining profitability and further growth.

Look at the top businesses in the world. Why are they so successful? Is it by chance? No. It is because they knew how to provide value to their target market, and soon everything ran on autopilot for them. They established a brand reputation and earned the trust of millions. This makes it easier for them to market their products and services and compounds their millions into billions. It is all part of a long-term but well-organized business strategy. When you hear stories of entrepreneurs failing after they invested money in them, you can find loads of reasons that hit the nail on the head: "Ah! This is why they got it wrong." These are what you call case studies, and case studies are the best way to analyze the success or failure of each business. You will study their business strategy and process, and then learn about their mentality regarding growth or dealing with unforeseeable circumstances.

Indeed, there are always external factors which are totally out of our control, but most of these successes and failures are determined by what we can control. And this is what we are going to learn about in-depth in this book. I will share with you one of the biggest reasons why my businesses thrived, as well as why you should patiently dedicate some time to planning before taking action. This piece of insight that granted me success was a document called the business plan. The business plan was the start of my unbelievable journey, and it changed my life within a couple of years. This book will explain the process for that first crucial element in my success story.

What This Book Will Teach You

This book will teach you about business plans. A business plan is a detailed document that explains a business's goals and objectives. Its purpose is to depict how the business will be run, how its marketing will be done, what financial resources are required, how employees will be managed, etc. You will find not only startups but also established firms using business plans. It is your manual for achieving greatness and, most importantly, creating your pitch for angel investors and those who will help you fund your business. A business plan is a presentation of all the facets involved in your business, and the more people you can impress with this document, the more you will see you are on the right track already.

I know some of you are reading this and getting excited about learning how to write a business plan, and some of you are feeling a little anxious about it. If you are the latter, don't worry, it is quite natural. I was in the same boat when I started writing one. I delayed getting something down on paper, and I felt like a rookie entrepreneur. What did I know about the fundamentals of a business and what elements should go into a business plan? I was so much of a perfectionist that I wanted to make sure I crafted a business plan that guaranteed profitability; hence, I procrastinated with writing one. The difference for you is that you have this book, which is going to remove all those fears and save you the time and frustration of trying to write a business plan without the proper knowledge.

In this book, you will learn the fundamentals of what a business should be all about, and these principles will be illustrated along the way as you prepare a business plan from scratch. You won't feel burdened by this step—which is a crucial part of your entrepreneurial journey—because we will explain the process in a linear way. As you read this book, you will get to know how each element of a business plan is vital to your pitch and how this can save you time and help you achieve profitability down the road.

All your worries about creating a business plan will go away as you learn the information broken down into chunks; this way, you will not miss out on any crucial detail. This book is designed to be your personal handbook that you can carry with you and refer to whenever you have a question or need a reminder. You will be able to visualize the template and create important, chronological details in your business plan as you are introduced to real-life lessons from case studies. You will see how some got it wrong and how some got it totally right.

Get Ready to Create a Document That Will Change Your Life

This was such an important part in my journey, and I want to share with you how creating a business plan took care of most of the things I worried about with starting my businesses because I gave this document top priority. I respected my plan, and by sticking with it, I was soon able to manage many successful businesses. And furthermore, I used this document to implement changes and expansion plans to grow my businesses based on the current market climate and the potential opportunities I saw. I adopted a growth mindset because I wanted my business plan to continue working for me and guiding me toward success. I used it as a reference document that I could easily update in order to plan expansions and grow beyond what I thought possible. This is the beauty of a business plan, and creating one is a skill you will put into practice again and again.

Once you understand the fundamentals of creating a great business plan, making more will come naturally and with ease. You can learn the systematic process for creating one, and you don't need any prior knowledge or experience with owning a business to get started. So, without further ado, let us dive straight in. I wish you a pleasant and life-changing read.

Chapter 1

Introduction to a Business Plan

Your value will be not what you know; it will be what you share.

— Ginni Rometty

We will start off the first chapter of this book by learning more about a business plan. Once again, a business plan is a crucial document that details all the information about how a business will get started and grow toward profitability. This chapter will go through the different business models which you can use as a foundation to create your own business plan. Moreover, you will learn why it is so important to write a business plan in the first place as we explore key case studies. You will see how failing to plan properly and write a business plan leads many unfortunate entrepreneurs to failure in their business endeavors. This book will give you the knowledge to avoid this downfall.

Second, you will also learn about the importance of planning in your entrepreneurial journey and how careful and purposeful planning can help you see those healthy profitable returns in the years to come. Furthermore, we will instill that strategic mentality to help you combat resistance along the way and adapt to changes around you, which will help create stability and ensure your business is in good shape for the long haul, churning out profit year in and year out. Let's dive in.

Business Models

Before we learn why we need to write a business plan, let us talk more about the profit-making machine that is what we call a business. For that, you will need to know what a business model is. A business model simply refers to the company's plan for making profits. It illustrates the products and services that it will offer and to which target audience in the market. Identifying and sticking to a business model is crucial for any company, whether new or established. Once you have a basic idea of what your business model is, this helps you to carry out other business-related activities, such as recruiting diverse talent for specific roles, attracting investments from various sources, deploying management, and devising an effective hierarchy in the organization.

This is extremely crucial for startup businesses but even more important for established ones. Think about it. Mature companies should be constantly updating their business model, or they will fall behind the market trends and their competition. Also, when it comes to the external stakeholders such as investors, it helps them to better analyze and judge a business's potential growth. You may know all about that if you've learned about the stock market and how investors and many investing gurus analyze certain companies and predict which dividend stock (distribution of a company's profits to its shareholders) or IPO (Initial Public Offering, where companies start launching their shares to the public) will be worth an investment. In most cases, they study the company's business model by using fundamental analysis and learning whether a business has the right ingredients to compete in the market and offer what people want.

In a nutshell, a business model is a business's core planning and strategic outline that shows how they will make profit. When it comes to any marketplace on this planet, understanding your business model is crucial high-level planning for running a business and, most importantly, making it a profitable one. You are making it clear to internal and external stakeholders, in plain language, what products or services will be sold, the clients you will engage, your business process, how you are different from your competitors, and much more.

Determining a Successful Business Model

Now, you may wonder, what makes a business model successful? In a nutshell, a successful business model allows you to meet clients' expectations, solve their problems at a competitive price, and provide them with value. It is all about taking your clients to their desired destination. You should take your clients from A to Z, with Z being the better version of what they had yesterday. Coming back to investors, they evaluate how a business model makes money so they can estimate what good financial growth will look like for the company.

Knowing how a successful business model works is not difficult. You can see many entrepreneurs making mistakes when
creating business models when they underestimate how much
funding the business will need before they see profits. They
fail to prepare for the long run. It is evident that a business
has to maintain itself until it makes enough revenue to offset
its expenses and initial investment.

Talking in pure financial terms, this is usually evaluated by
going through a business's gross profit. As you know,
revenue means the income a company makes via sales of
their products and services. Then there is "cost of goods
sold," or COGS in short. This is the total cost or expense the
company bears in producing the product or service they
deliver to the clients. So, subtracting the COGS from the
revenue gives you the gross profit of a company. On the other
hand, you also have cash flow, which investors like to
analyze if they find the gross profit not convincing enough in
their analysis. Cash flow is basically the gross profit minus
the operating expenses, which ultimately gives you how
much profit they are generating from their model. To sum it
all up, it is simple when you look to balance two key indicators—cost and pricing.

When a company is able to provide a product or service and
can raise prices and find ways to lower the cost of producing
them, the company is on to a great business model. It is all
about finding that model that offers the flexibility to balance
these two indicators. When you find a business model that
proves to be successful and everything is set in place properly, it can later be operated on autopilot mode, which
requires a minimum level of management.

Types of Business Models

Now that you have a good understanding of the importance of a successful business model, let us go through some specific types of business models. In other words, different types of businesses. You can find business models that are of the traditional nature and also hybrid ones that combine both worlds of brick-and-mortar and online stores to enhance and diversify their client outreach.

Here are a few you will probably recognize instantly and others to refresh your memory:

1. **Retailer Model**

A retailer business model is probably the most commonly implemented business model out there. A retailer is the last point in the supply chain and ends up interacting with the customer the most. A typical retailer model involves sourcing goods from manufacturers, wholesalers, and distributors and supplying them directly to the consumers. Examples of famous retailers include Amazon, Walmart, and Costco.

2. **Manufacturer**

Manufacturers are mainly responsible for producing raw materials or finished goods by utilizing different input sources such as machinery, labor, and other materials. Manufacturers are specialized in producing finished goods at a maximum speed using a systemized manufacturing process and getting them ready to be shipped to various wholesalers, distributors, and retailers. They may even sell products directly to end consumers. Examples of famous manufacturers include automobile giants such as Ford Motor Company and Toyota.

3. Service-Based Model

The last two business models were examples of producing and selling products. What if you wanted to sell a service? That's where a fee-for-service business model suits you. This is all about utilizing labor and providing services for clients. The service model can be a fee charged on an hourly basis or a fixed fee for a specific task or project. The deliverables, duration, and other conditions are usually outlined in an agreement before delivery of service. This is a sophisticated business model to carry out because it requires the training of staff and being consistent with the quality of service that is delivered day after day.

4. Subscription-Based Model

This business model is all about a subscription-based system that sells clients on a long-term commitment. This can be done by providing a product or service in exchange for recurring payments for a fixed duration of providing that value benefit. These are usually practiced by tech companies, especially SaaS businesses (Software as a Service). Moreover, it is a popular model for providing physical goods, such as agricultural products, and equipment for a fixed time period. An example of a popular subscription giant would be Spotify.

5. Freemium Business Model

This business model is quite different from the other business models we've covered so far. It introduces customers to products that offer limited scope. Basically, the strategy is to give customers only a small portion of value until they start craving more. Hence, after a customer begins using the service or product and decides they want more from it, like better features and no limitations, businesses can lure them into signing up for premium versions, where they get access to all the benefits for a price. This model nurtures customers by giving them a taste of the product or service before finally converting them into a long-term paying client. Examples of this model include LinkedIn and Spotify.

6. **Bundling Model**

Some businesses practice selling a bundle of products or services to individual clients. This is called bundling, and this happens when a business feels there is less scope for attracting many customers without spending lots of money to attract them in the first place. So, they try to capitalize on each client by selling different products and services all at once at competitive prices, usually bargain deals and discounts. AT&T is a good example of a business practicing this specific business model.

7. **Marketplace**

You may have heard of marketplaces in the context of a place where freelancers and companies offer services, but they've actually been around for a long time. Dating back to the advent of the traditional business model of trade and barter, marketplaces physically existed so various merchants could conduct business and receive their desired compensation. Fast forward to today, and you now find online marketplaces, which are basically platforms hosted for businesses to do their thing: reaching out to buyers, carrying out transactions, and delivering products or services. As a result, it makes the transaction much easier and quicker. It is also much safer. Examples of marketplaces you see online are eBay, Etsy, Fiverr, and Upwork.

8. Affiliate-Based Model

You might have heard of something called affiliate marketing. In this business model, an individual or company markets another entity's products or services to others for a small piece of the profit pie. Many companies pay a good fee to affiliates who carry out these promotions successfully, and this is quite scalable, as it all depends on how many people the affiliate can reach in exchange for commissions. You see this commonly practiced by social media influencers online, where they promote different products for a company and ask their followers to purchase them using an affiliate link so that they can receive a small commission once the buyer makes the purchase.

9. Razor Blade Business Model

The razor blade model basically aims to sell a product that has high versatility and durability below a price range in the hopes of generating high sales numbers and profit. The razor blade moniker came into use when razor blade companies gave blade handles to consumers knowing they would need to buy blades regularly to shave. An example of a company that uses the razor blade model is the tech company Hewlett-Packard, with the way they sell their printers.

10. Reverse Razor Blade Business Model

If you thought it ended with the razor blade, then you will be surprised to learn that there is another model that's quite the opposite. So, a razor blade model looks to sell a low-margin product to consumers in high volume. But a reverse razor blade model aims to sell a high-margin product directly. As a result, you will find products that are of high upfront value but low in durability. An example of a company that practices this business model is Apple when selling their iPhones.

11. Franchise Model

Franchising basically means giving rights to a franchisor to reproduce the company's business and offer the same products and services in different locations and target markets. In this arrangement, the franchisor receives a percentage of the earnings from the franchisee. The franchise model has been here for many years, and this helps a business to expand to different locations, especially for global presence and exposure. Common franchises include fast-food giants such as McDonalds, Domino's Pizza, and Burger King.

12. Pay-as-You-Go Model

As you have learned, some companies charge fixed fees for their products and services. But there is a business model where you can charge depending on how much the product or service is utilized. This probably reminds you of utility companies, and yes, they use this business model by charging a fee that is commensurate with how much electricity, water, etc., we use each month. You will find businesses today using this business model to get an idea of how much a client uses their products and services and then offering compensation based on those numbers.

13. **Brokerage Model**

Lastly, a business model like the brokerage basically entails a middleman who helps to connect various buyers with sellers. Make note that this is different from marketplaces. You do not need a marketplace to practice a brokerage business model. A brokerage company receives a percentage of the amount after the deal is closed. You will find this business model commonly practiced in real estate.

Choosing Your Business Model

After learning about the different types of business models, it may seem overwhelming to try to choose from so many options, and you may be wondering how to go about it for your own business idea. To avoid all that unease, let me take you through a step-by-step process that will make your job easier. Once you've decided on which business model to use, you can begin to plan and fully commit to your model with confidence. Here is how you can take it one step at a time:

Step 1: Identify the target audience.

The first step is to determine your audience. This is crucial to identify before thinking about what problem you are going to solve because you will need to target the right people and commit to it. A bad business model will result in a mismatch of products/services and the target market that these products/services are aimed at. You don't want to solve a problem for a group of people who don't actually have the problem and aren't looking for a solution. Hence, it is important to know who you are targeting from the beginning so that you can wisely move on to the next step, which is knowing how to connect with your target market.

Step 2: Define the problem.

Now you will need to think through the problem you are trying to solve. Assess your target market's pain points and the problems that keep them up at night, then store all that information in writing to build upon as you go. Broadly speaking, one problem might be when a population is hungry and doesn't have a lot of places to go eat. Hence, they need more food offerings, so a restaurant opens up in their area to solve that pain point. Another example might be a business district without a lot of office suppliers around. What do they do when they need a bulk order of pens? Soon, an office supplies store opens up in the area offering a solution to their problem.

Step 3: Create your offerings.

Now that you know the problem you are going to solve, plan out how you can solve it. Your offer or solution might consist of products or services. Ensure that you understand the type of offer you are putting out there and, most importantly, know how you will be able to offer it regularly and consistently to your target market.

Step 4: Assess internal requirements.

Once you have defined your target market, their problem, and your offering, you will need to list out specific challenges, which include your operational costs, processes, and management-related activities that can help leverage or limit your business. It is useful here to identify and document all these requirements so that you will know what your business model will require ahead of time to effectively function and keep delivering value to your target audience.

Step 5: Determine profit generation.

In the end of it all, your business exists to make money, and I believe you like hearing the word "profit." In this step, you will need to define how the company will make its money by planning a business strategy that balances out the two key indicators—price and cost—which we covered earlier. You will need a long-term plan to keep meeting customer requirements and expectations.

Step 6: Gather key stakeholders.

It is a known fact that most businesses need investors or partners that can help take them to another level of startup capital to make sure the business can smoothly transition from a startup to a profitable company. You will definitely need to partner with many people, such as suppliers, investors, and brands, to get the funding, raw materials, sponsorship deals, etc., to turn your business into a money-making machine. Therefore, identify your key partners and stakeholders that you will need to play a part in your business, then prioritize your relationship with them so you don't waste your resources elsewhere.

Step 7: Execute.

Last but not least, after planning your business model, it is time to put it into practice. Test it out by asking people in your target market how they would perceive this business and whether they would buy your products and services. Basically, you will need to carry out surveys and additional research to back up your business model and evaluate your chances of success. For this, feedback is so important, especially from the market you are serving.

Remember that you shouldn't feel pressured to find the "perfect business model" out there. Some will work, and some won't be the right fit for you. Many unsuccessful business models fail because their core planning and story didn't make sense. You will need to study the steps we've just learned, and then you will see why unsuccessful business models fall short.

Also, an important tip I would like to add, apart from the importance of creating a good business model, is to pay attention to market factors by analyzing the market. You can do this by utilizing something called PESTEL analysis, which will be discussed in-depth later in the book, and knowing your competition inside and out. If you can do this, you will be moving in the right direction toward creating a business model that will turn into a profitable and sustainable venture.

The Importance of Writing a Business Plan

Moving on to business plans, here are a few reasons why you should write yours with an almost religious fervor and treat it as the key factor in determining your business's success or failure.

Presenting Yourself as a Serious Phenomenon

First and foremost, having a business plan creates the first impression that you are someone who is here and ready to play the game. You are not here to mess around, and you do mean business (apologies for the pun). A business plan is formal in nature and functions as a way to present your business in a clean, professional manner to interested stakeholders and potential investors. Having a good business plan in place will also do wonders for your own confidence in your endeavor. Yes, you are showing yourself that you are serious about the whole thing, and there is something psychologically amazing about writing things down with a purpose. You will find it easy to commit to your plan if it is well executed. Writing down a business plan from scratch is such a motivational boost for anyone. It shouldn't feel like a chore. You are using it as a way to start your engine and move forward. A business plan serves as your anchor and will help you see the path toward success. We all know that having a plan helps alleviate the usual anxieties and fears that come along with taking risks, so don't be lazy with this step.

Establishing Important Milestones for Your Business

Another major reason why you should write a business plan is for long-term purposes. It may sound intimidating when you are thinking about starting a big business. You might only be thinking about the end goal of becoming a profitable business, and this is where many end up tripping up. You must see this as a journey where there are different milestones to pass on the way to that desired destination you're dreaming about. Hence, a business plan is a great way to plan your long-term goals by breaking them up into small business milestones that are more digestible and achievable in your eyes. The key is to take it one step at a time; moreover, milestones are celebratory achievements for entrepreneurs, and you should look forward to reaching them so you can enjoy mini successes along the way in your entrepreneurial journey. Furthermore, milestones provide a progressive direction for where you will take your business in the years to come. It is another way to reverse engineer your business's success by learning what steps or milestones are needed to reach your desired goal.

Understanding More About Your Target Market

The next important reason why you should write a business plan is to understand your target market or customers better. You will be analyzing their buying habits, such as knowing when they tend to buy and why they end up buying what you are offering. Remember that everything to do with your business's success is centered around customer satisfaction. If you keep your customers satisfied by fulfilling their needs in a timely manner, then you are doing a pretty good job, and there is nothing else you need to worry about. Don't try to fix something that isn't broken. When you know your customers better, it helps you to produce better products and service strategies. This knowledge will help you make important decisions to improve your performance, like finding ways to adjust the pricing and cost of producing your products and services. Moreover, knowing more about your audience helps you to carry out marketing campaigns effectively because you will know what inspires them to action and makes your product or service stand out to them. The goal is to have your target market always thinking of your business first when they have a specific need.

Don't Forget That Your Competition Matters, Too

Understanding your target market is one thing, but knowing your competition is another important reason why you should have a solid business plan in place. In any industry, there is competition. In some industries, there are fewer competitors, and in others, there are loads of them. You can decide whether a market is saturated or not based on the level of competition you see. Hence, it is crucial to know your competition's strengths and weaknesses in detail so you can evaluate how your business can come in and compete with them. One good lesson is to not fear your competition but use them as a source for understanding how your business can profit from the industry. Carrying out a competitive analysis will prepare you in advance to tackle hardships in the market and give you the inspiration to provide better offerings for your customers. I prefer to think of it in this way.

Evaluate the Possibilities of Your Venture

Writing a business plan helps you assess whether you are on to a good opportunity or not. Hence, this acts as a risk mitigation technique and reduces the likelihood that you will jump head-first into a business idea that is doomed to fail. You are putting in hours writing a business plan and conducting various market research strategies to learn about your competition, craft your offer, and run your business. This preparation can help you to bring forward your previous assumptions about a certain business model or target market that may prove to be incorrect following your research. You can then change your opinion and plans regarding these factors. From a situation where you thought your idea was going to be complicated and unpopular, you may flip the switch and realize that you are on to a great venture here based on your research findings. You will feel more optimistic about finding buyers when the research shows what they are looking for. It's definitely a win-win situation to write a business plan in my eyes, and you should feel the same.

Financial Reasons for Why You Need a Business Plan

Writing a business plan simply gives you a clear idea of how much capital you will require and helps you determine where you can go about looking for these funds. This is important because startup capital can vary based on your business model, the industry, and the target market you are reaching out to. Based on how much capital you require, your sources of capital will vary, too. Moreover, you will need to determine how your business is going to make money. When you outline this information in a business plan, you will be given a canvas on which to express your ideas, and trust me, you will be amazed at the ideas and problem-solving skills you hone as you craft your revenue model for your business. So, write out your profit-making model and be sure you understand the challenges you could face that might limit your profitability. Also, it is wise to consider more revenue streams and not solely think from a one-dimensional standpoint. For example, if you are planning to sell software in your business, don't just think of gaining revenue from your software sales. Think about how you can bring in revenue from brand deals, affiliates, and much more.

Attraction is the Power of Business Plans

You probably know this by now, but again, I would like to remind you that your business plan is the hub of attraction for your potential investors, employees, partners, etc. When it comes to presenting something convincing and exciting to investors, your formal business plan is the foundation from which you will launch your exciting and convincing pitch. A very good business plan speaks for itself by addressing all the investors' questions and objections while also boosting their interest. It also does the work of attracting business partners who will join your business venture after reading the detailed description of your business model and being sold on your dream. When it comes to attracting employees and senior heads for your business, having a business plan helps to guide you in recruiting the right talent. It will also help you retain your talent through a harmonious and productive organizational culture, while you attract more talent during your expansion stage. Therefore, a solid business plan can indirectly motivate your employees and get them producing positive results that will directly aid in your company's growth.

A Great Source of Documentation

Business plans are also simply that secured anchor where you will keep a record of anything important regarding your business. You can document your revenue models and determine which one can earn the highest profits. You can record your marketing plan in detail by stating how you will engage with your customers, sell them your offer, and keep winning repeat buyers. Documenting all your strategies and tactics will help you when it comes time to revisit them and implement updated measures for the current market. Moreover, you can use it to learn more about your business's manpower requirements by documenting and improving your strategy for recruiting and training talent, which will hopefully encourage them to stay for the long haul.

Planning Your Entrepreneurial Journey

Business planning is the antidote for removing all that fear and self-doubt. For me, this was the case, anyway. All the planning helped me stay better informed, and I gradually felt more in control of running the business even though I didn't start it straightaway. Having these foundations in place helps to motivate you and make you believe in the project. A good business plan doesn't work to convince others first, but in fact will instill confidence in yourself and your business venture. Without confidence in yourself, you'll never be able to convince others of your potential success.

It is quite natural for an entrepreneur to feel a bit of anxiety and maybe even pessimistic about the whole thing. But this is due to lack of clarity and the uncertainty that surrounds those fears. These all can be solved by executing business planning and gaining insight, then working on your problem-solving skills to craft solution models that will convince you that this opportunity is the right one to pursue. Every entrepreneur's journey starts with overcoming that fear and feeling of impending failure. Those who overcome it go on to achieve great things because they never gave up before they even began the race, and then stayed the course.

Your Actions Speak

Aspiring entrepreneurs are good at creating the perfect business idea but then failing to execute it. If this sounds like you, you may feel hurt, but I am just pointing out hard truths. It is all about taking action, and every entrepreneur's journey is about action. Execution is the key to your success and relishing every moment in your journey. After months of making progress, you will realize in time that the work you put in during the previous months is the sole reason why you are standing after achieving one of your business milestones or reaching that ultimate goal you always dreamed of. Taking each step in that action plan is the reason you've gained experience, learned from your mistakes, overcome the fear of risk, and gone after your dreams. Hence, it is crucial to focus on executing your ideas by taking action immediately rather than just visualizing it in your head day in and day out without putting yourself out into the world.

Build a Team of Reliable Talent

A conscientious entrepreneur is good when it comes to managing people and knowing who he or she needs to help execute the business plan. There are solopreneurs out there, but they don't necessarily get things done alone or do everything by themselves. They still collaborate with other people, partner with brands, and achieve the goals they set for themselves. You cannot find success alone without the help of the people around you. An entrepreneur needs people to succeed, and this is important to understand when starting a business and looking to maintain a successful venture. When you write down your business plan, this is a great time to craft your hiring plan and get an idea of what type of talent you will need to recruit to help manage the expectations of your team. Moreover, it is a great place to plan how you will retain your talent and utilize their skills to see your dream come to fruition while making everyone happy and satisfied within your company.

Set Financial Goals

In the heart of every entrepreneur's passion, there also lies the intellectual ability to take money seriously and understand the importance of finance in a business. Any entrepreneur should prioritize financial goals that are well-defined and which outline achievable milestones on the road to your ultimate business goal—making profits. Therefore, in your journey, you must treat your money with respect by implementing cost-effective measures and producing high-quality products or services that fulfill your clients' needs. Doing this successfully will naturally lead to a situation where you can raise prices and still retain buyers. Financial goals help you to scale your business better in the long run and avoid the trap of failed business ventures due to poor financial planning.

When it comes to planning your entrepreneurial journey, it is all about understanding your psychology. You have to stay optimistic, even though this is easier said than done. Failure is never the end of the world, but it isn't something that you can afford when you are taking big risks in your life. A good business plan will help buffer you against making mistakes or poorly thought-out actions due to insufficient knowledge and planning. As you see those small successes piling up, this will help you maintain faith in your project and lessen the common anxieties faced by entrepreneurs. So, never let failure pull you down. Learn from it and let those insights help you build a better plan that will give you every reason to succeed. Your new plan will act as a guide you can refer to, like a roadmap to success. Always use the data to help you make decisions rather than acting impulsively.

Before moving on to the next chapter, I would like to mention that you always should try to avoid comparing your entrepreneurial journey with someone else's. Everyone's journey is different—let it be personal or business. One might start a business when they are 20, and there are others who start relatively late in life, in their 60s, and yet both can be successful because they focused on their journey and didn't let another's journey intimidate or discourage them. Always commit to your journey and write your story for yourself.

Key Takeaways From This Chapter

- A business model is basically a strategic plan to show how your business will make money. This mainly includes illustrating the products or services you will offer and what type of problem you are solving for your specific target market.
- There are many types of business models you can choose from, including retailers, manufacturers, service-based, subscription-based, Freemium, bundling, marketplace, affiliate-based, razor blade,

reverse razor blade, franchise, pay-as-you-go, and brokerage.

- Many top companies utilize different business models. For example, Walmart is a top retail company. Spotify utilizes the freemium and subscription business models. Real estate companies largely practice the brokerage business model.
- You can create a successful business model by following crucial steps, and these are: identifying a target market, defining their problem, crafting a strong solution or offer, assessing internal requirements, assessing finances, finding the right partners, and testing out your model by acquiring more information using surveys.
- Writing a business plan is important so that you can present yourself as a serious entrepreneur to your investors, employees, partners, etc. Moreover, a business plan is the best way to learn more about your project and convince yourself that you're headed in the right direction.

Chapter 2

How to Create a Business Plan

There are no secrets to success. It is the result of prepara-tion, hard work, and learning from failure.

— Colin Powell

This chapter is probably one of the most essential ones in the book, but it's important to not skip ahead. You should digest each section and example so that you are thoroughly understanding the key elements. You will want to learn the proper format for your business plan and be sure you're including all the necessary details. We will go through each part of the business plan in this chapter, and along the way, you will be immersed in insights for what you need to include in each section of your business plan alongside examples of that section. Therefore, by the end of this chapter, you will be ready to craft your own business plan correctly.

So, I would recommend getting a pen and paper for this chapter because you will need to really digest all of these elements we are going to learn about. In this chapter, we will cover the traditional business plan format that has been used for many years. It is basically the most detailed way to do things. It does take more time to write this format; however, we do this so that all the details are clear to whomever is reading them. If you want to present a fine business pitch to potential investors, you will need to master writing a traditional business plan. Other types of business plan formats include the "lean startup plan," which focuses more on illustrating only key elements and takes less time to write. The downside to using this format is that investors may not get as good an idea of the business and they may request more information after reading it.

Table of Contents Page

Coming back to writing the traditional business plan, it is super important to stick with the format, with the elements in the right order, and to include the right information in each section. Many investors and funders have read countless business plans from various entrepreneurs, so it is usually best to maintain the same format that those people are used to reading. Surprises can be good, but what I've learned is that mimicking the successful and generally accepted strategy in this regard is helpful for the sake of the readers' comfort and familiarity. Don't waste your energy trying to be original and impressive yet; you've got to reel them in first. In the end, you are preparing a business plan for them to read and get an idea of what your business is all about; they're not looking for how fancy or creative you can be.

First and foremost, you need to have a cover page that displays your business name in large font and labels the packet as a business plan. Then, inside the plan, you need to include your Table of Contents page. This is where you will lay out all the section headers and subheadings (optional) along with their page numbers to assist the reader. Some readers prefer to go straight to the financial section rather than reading the market analysis page (like bankers would when deciding whether to grant loans), so it is crucial to have this reference page available. Now, let us go through each major section one by one for what needs to be covered in a business plan.

The Executive Summary

When a reader reads a novel, they are often given a small section called the introduction. This is where special considerations about the novel are summarized into a few blocks of text, giving readers a clear picture of what they are about to read. Similarly, when it comes to presenting a business plan, it can be intimidating at first for any reader to see a fat copy of your business plan with a lot of pages to read. For that, you need a small summary to tell your reader what your business is all about and why it will be successful.

Your Executive Summary should be written on the first page of your business plan; hence, this is going to be touched upon first. Note that everything will be explained in a linear fashion to help you write your business plan in the right order and strictly stick with the format. Treat your Executive Summary as your elevator pitch. You are pitching your idea to the reader straightaway, and in this area, first impression is very important.

The main elements of a summary include a description of your product or service offerings, a mission statement, and a brief plan for your financial growth. It is crucial that you make a good first impression on your summary so that investors or any other reader will like the idea straightaway and feel more interested in reading your entire business plan.

How to Structure Your Executive Summary

Your Executive Summary should be short, but you will need to include all the necessary details in that short section, so it is crucial to understand what you need to include. Here is what you should include in your Executive Summary:

Write a hook.

Your first sentence or paragraph is basically your hook. You are reeling your readers into what your business plan is all about. You want their attention, so you don't want them to get bored straight off the bat. Hence, you need to add a bit of personality to your hook and share a brief description of what you're setting your eyes on. It might be the problem you are looking to solve which will entice the readers to learn more about you and what you are presenting as a solution to that problem in the form of your business.

Write the company description summary.

After writing the hook, you should write a brief introduction to your company. Don't make it too long, but write in simple language what your business does and what you are going to offer. Typically, a company description will include basic information regarding the business, such as when and why it was formed, where you are going to conduct your business, all the products and services you are going to offer, who you are going to offer them to, and the names of the founders or executives that will play a role in your company.

Write a market analysis.

Next up, you will need to write a brief section that includes your market analysis and shows how well-prepared you are. Show that you've gained the necessary knowledge about the competing markets and that you are ready to take this business forward. You should mention who your competitors are, the level of demand for your offerings, and how you can stand out in this market amidst other competitors. Remember to only include the necessary and important highlights regarding the market analysis in this section, as this can tend to run on too long.

Write about your products and services.

Next up, write about your offerings. Highlight what products and services your business will offer and list out any other important sales and growth strategy plans for your company. Remember, it is good to show how your company is unique, so highlight how your product or service will satisfy a need in your target market in a different or superior way to that already being offered by your competitors.

Write your financial information.

Next, you will need to write about your business's financial goals. Remember that you can go in-depth about this later in your business plan, so it is best to just include the highlights here as a basic overview. You can include a few figures to paint a clearer picture if you want, and also mention what type of funding you are looking for. Moreover, this is the best place to state estimated projections so that you can impress potential investors and begin convincing them that you are thinking big and that you have the business model to back up your claims.

Write your future plans.

It is important to show that you are in it for the long run and that you are thinking ahead. Write down what your plan is for using startup funds, as this is crucial—especially when an investor or any other funder is reading your business plan cold. They may be interested and probably a bit anxious to know what you will do with their money, so you will need to articulately explain how you are going to use it. This is where you can include any expansion plans you have in mind, like opening in additional locations, expanding your product line, or spending more to carry out marketing campaigns. Hence, show that you think big, and make sure you tell the story to your readers regarding how you plan to get there. This will also show them how wise you can be in handling funds you are given, so this can be a crucial piece in the Executive Summary.

Writing a Good Executive Summary

It shouldn't be a tough task for you to write a good, brief summary of your business. You are promoting your own business idea and dream, after all. So, make sure you put your heart into it and share your passion with others around you. In addition, it is important that you follow a few tips to make sure you create the best possible Executive Summary.

Tip #1: Make it clear and concise.

As you already know, an Executive Summary is a brief description of your company information, so you don't need to write a lot of pages on it. You have less space to work with here, so make sure you include only the necessary information in this section. A good strategy is to write your summary concisely by avoiding using repetitive words or redundant information. Avoid words such as "that," commonly used clichés, superlatives, and facts that are not backed by research. Being strict with avoiding these irrelevant pieces of information is encouraged so that you end up with a clear and comprehensible summary. Use clear, simple language and avoid using too much business terminology that would confuse or bore your reader.

Tip #2: Utilize bullet points.

Using bullet points is a fine way to turn your large block of text into small, digestible chunks, making it easy for readers to scan your content. This is crucial for any reader who's in a hurry and wants to get straight to the point with your business summary without going further into the document. Having bullet points with short sentences or paragraphs simply makes the reading experience more pleasurable for those you are pitching to.

Tip #3: Focus on the strengths.

Your business plan must stand out, so to make it unique among all your competitors, you have to put emphasis on your business's strengths and convince the reader why your business is worth investing in or providing funding for. In brief, focusing on the strengths is a good way to get readers excited and invested in your project.

Tip #4: Focus on your reader.

Always remember who you are writing this Executive Summary for. You are writing it for your readers, who are most likely investors, business partners, employees, and other important potential stakeholders. You want to ensure they don't get bored by reading a business plan that is overly formal or verbose. Hence, you should personalize your summary by writing it as a human being and not making the content read like it was written by a robot. Most people make mistakes when writing a summary because they focus on the business investment while forgetting about enticing the readers. You can still be a bit creative and expressive in your summary, just enough to get your readers excited about the whole business venture. A lot depends on who you are speaking to and the industry you are working in.

Tip #5: Test it out.

After writing your summary, it is recommended that you get someone to read your draft. This can be someone working in your industry or a potential business partner. Make them read your summary and have them share their honest feedback regarding it. This is a great way to get more opinions on how to improve your summary rather than depending exclusively on your own opinion. You can also get support from online tools such as Grammarly to spell check and proofread your summary to make sure there are no typos or minor grammatical errors.

Tip #6: Consider writing your summary last.

This may sound strange, but you might also consider writing your summary after you've prepared the entire business plan. This will help you include all the key information you have written about in-depth and will make it easier to assemble those points and get all of them down in a brief summary. If you don't want to leave this section for last, you can always start writing your business plan by starting with the Executive Summary and later revisiting it after completing your business plan. Then, you can make changes that focus on creating an appealing and concise summary for your readers.

Example of an Executive Summary

Pet Food Inc.

Problem Statement

Many pet owners are finding it difficult to buy pet food for their pets due to their busy lifestyles and lack of pet food options in their locality. XX% of pet owners spend their income on buying pet food for their pets, but there is a lack of delivery services to deliver this pet food to them in a timely manner.

Value Proposition

Pet Food Inc. provides a fast and reliable pet food delivery service by utilizing an app. Pet owners can choose from a range of products and provide their pets with delicious and healthy food. Our team ensures that all pet owners can focus on their lives while we take care of delivering food for their pets on time.

Company Overview

Pet Food Inc. is located in Toronto. The company is owned by partners XXX and XXX. Both have experience working in sales and marketing. Both partners will take on the management roles in the company. In addition, there will be a board of advisors to assist them with the management duties. Advisors include XXX, XX, XX, and XXX.

Market Analysis

In Canada, there is huge demand for pet food, and the market research shows that pet owners shop regularly every week to provide food items for their pets. With the busy lifestyles of our app's users, it was shown that they don't have time to go out and get food for their pets themselves.

Products and Services

We provide pet food delivery services by offering an app that pet owners can use to order pet food and have it delivered quickly by our drivers. In addition, we offer other services, such as delivering pet care products and providing insight on pet care services in the user's current location. Despite there being many pet food providers in the area, our company stands out with its uniquely built app, which lets users instantly place orders and get their pet food delivered faster.

Future Plan

Pet Food Inc. is aiming to partner with pet food stores and companies in the first year. Our target is to sign up at least 10 pet food stores per month. By the end of the second year, we plan to have broadened our exposure and opened offices in Kingston and Hamilton—extending our pet food delivery services and app exposure to these two cities.

Financial Requirements and Projections

For startup finances, we are looking to have an operating line of $XXX in our first year. The partners together have invested around $XXX to meet those requirements. Based on the market research data and projections, we estimate our sales for the first year to be around $XXX, at a growth rate of XX%. Each partner will receive a salary of $XXX, and we aim to sign around XXX clients in the first few months.

Company Description

After writing the Executive Summary, it is time to go in-depth with describing your company. In this section, you should include essential information, such as your official business name you have registered, the official address of where your business is located, and the key names of the people who will play a part in your business.

This is also the best place to write about your business's legal structure—whether you are a sole proprietorship, partnership, corporation, or LLC. Here is a brief explanation of these legal structures so you get the idea:

- **Sole proprietorship**: This is the simplest and most common type of business legal structure, as it is only owned by one individual.
- **Partnership**: A partnership is an association of two or more people who own the business and share the profits amongst themselves.
- **Corporation**: Corporations are the most complex business legal structure, as they consist of individuals or shareholders who form the business entity.
- **Limited Liability Company (LLC)**: This is a hybrid of the corporation and partnership legal structures, as it also involves an association of individuals or members who form the business entity.

Of course, legal structures can differ based on your country, so do a little bit of research for wherever you are located or talk to your legal advisor to get more information on which legal structure you need to form your business. In every legal structure, there needs to be a statement outlining the percentage of ownership each owner has and their involvement in the business. Moreover, you should write in-depth about the history of your company and why you decided to form it. This is a good indicator for your potential readers or investors, as it will help them get to know which direction you want the business to head in.

In a nutshell, your company description is a basic overview regarding the background of your company to offer a clear understanding of how your business entity exists.

The Importance of Having a Company Description

In any pitch, it is crucial to introduce yourself. Most people are not willing to buy from a stranger, regardless of how great the offer is. They need to know who they are dealing with and get a clear idea of who you are and what your vision is. The company description acts as just that, as it reveals all the basic information regarding your business. It is important to place this right after the Executive Summary page because your readers—whether they are investors, partners, employees, etc.—need to know who you are. This is even more important when you approach lenders because they absolutely need to know what your company is all about and what your history is before they lend you any amount of money. Hence, to win lenders, investors, and other potential stakeholders, a company description is necessary to present a clear picture of your business.

To summarize, this is what you need to include in your company description:

- basic company information, such as your registered business name, legal structure, and business location
- ownership information and other details regarding your management
- history and background of your company
- mission statement that exhibits what type of problem you are solving
- overview of the products and services you will provide and to which type of customers

Example of a Company Description

Here is a sample of a company overview that may give you some inspiration. Of course, you can always write a bit more in-depth, as this can only improve the effect on your readers.

Mark's Work Supplies

Ownership Structure

Mark's Work Supplies is a business formed to deliver office supplies to small-to-medium-sized businesses in Canada. The business structure is a partnership co-owned by partners Mark and his wife Elysha. The percentage of ownership will be XX% for Mark and XX% for Elysha. The company is located in Kingston, Ontario. It is expected to begin its operation this May.

Company History and Background

Mark's Work Supplies was formed in the year 20XX. Mark has vast experience working in the office furniture industry, having worked for top giants such as XXX and XXX in his XX years of experience. Elysha has experience working in XXX as a supply chain manager in her XX years in the office supplies industry. Both will combine their experience and skill sets to form a business and deliver office supplies to businesses.

Mission

The company identifies the potential need for office supplies delivery to busy businesses, including such essentials as paper, ink, pens, envelopes, and also hardware solutions like printers, computers, scanners, projectors, etc. Mark's Work Supplies aims to be a fast office supplies delivery service which will have a competitive advantage over other rivals who take longer to deliver bulk orders.

The company is aiming to have gross sales of about $XXX by the end of its first year and over $XXX in sales after five years. Mark's Work Supplies is also looking to expand its services later on to provide software solutions to businesses by partnering with software companies across Canada.

Market Analysis

Any potential lender or investor will want to know how your business's products or services will stand out against other competitors in the market. To lay this out, you will need to include a market analysis section in your business plan. This section will explain all about who your target market is and the numbers regarding the demand for your solution. It should also discuss who your competitors are, their strengths and weaknesses, and how you will position yourself in a competitive market.

You can conduct market research by using the internet and the local chamber of commerce, conducting surveys, analyzing competitors, and using other reliable resources to write your market analysis.

What Do I Include in a Market Analysis?

In a market analysis, you should include the following information:

Objective

First and foremost, you will need to begin your market analysis by defining your objective and outlining the problem you are going to solve with your business. There are two kinds of objectives you can focus on. One is to conduct a market analysis to find new products or services to launch in the existing marketplace. The other is to do enough market analysis to get a business loan approved. Hence, your objective for writing a market analysis is important and should be mentioned before anything else.

Industry Overview

The next detail to include in your market analysis is your industry overview. You will need to explain your understanding of the industry and where it is heading. Is there a good growth forecast in the industry that backs your intent of running a business in the first place? This information will give you a good idea of whether you are way ahead of the market or too late to the party regarding certain products and services. For instance, you would find it extremely difficult to sell DVDs or DVD players when people can access streaming services online for a small subscription fee. In your industry overview, include the size of the market using statistics and figures from credible sources. You can also mention your product's expected life cycle in the industry, its projected growth, and the major factors that you believe will lead to that growth rate.

Target Market

Your next section in the market analysis should be all about who your customers are. Who is your potential target audience, really? And how would you describe your ideal customer? Answering these questions is important to learn all about who you are selling to and how you can cater your offer to solve their specific problems. The industry plays a part in identifying who your target customers are and understanding their buying habits. You should include demographic information such as age, gender, income level, lifestyle, etc. Identify your ideal customer's persona and provide research materials like surveys from focus groups to back up your research.

Market Value

You will also want to include statistical data and figures in your market analysis to convince the reader and support your claims, enticing them to buy into the business opportunity you are pursuing. These numbers may include an evaluation of how many people there are who are buying a particular product in the market and your projections regarding sales. This analysis is a good way to gain an understanding of your market, the most popular products being sold, competitors' pricing strategy, and consumers' buying habits and trends.

Competition

You can include the expected level of competition in your market by analyzing the market share of leaders in your specific market. In this section, you will need to examine two types of competitors—direct and indirect competition. Direct competitors are your directly competing businesses who sell the same product or service as you do. On the other hand, your indirect competitors offer different products or services, but they are similar enough to yours that they can still potentially snatch your customers away. This is also the best place in your business plan to mention your competitors' strengths, weaknesses, and how you will stand out against them.

Barriers

While writing your market analysis, you will need to also identify some barriers that may inhibit your startup process. This is simply known as the "barrier of entry." Factors affecting a business's barrier of entry might include technology, brand strength, the cost to enter a market, and also the location. These factors will vary by industry, and so it is important to do your research and gain insight about your industry's specific barriers.

Laws and Regulations

It is also important to know the different laws and regulations relating to your industry in your location. The most commonly researched regulations include a market's employment and labor laws, tax codes, privacy laws, and environmental regulations. It is wise to do your research and also consult with your legal advisor to make sure you have all the information regarding the various laws and regulations that will directly impact you.

Example of a Market Analysis

Here is an example of how you can write your market analysis section in your business plan. Just like the above examples, this is only for inspiration, so feel free to add more information under each respective header.

Ben's RV Rentals

Problem to Solve

XX% of people living in the U.S. and Canada are interested in traveling and immersing themselves in "the van life." They enjoy spending time with their families, friends, and pets, and traveling the country. However, there are few places offering RV rentals near their localities for them to go to and rent an RV, and despite a good rate of production of RVs each year, there are fewer rental companies to connect these newer RVs with interested rental customers.

Industry

The RV (Recreational Vehicle) and camper industry is valued at around $XX and it is projected to reach about $XXX by 2028 at a CAGR of XX%. The emerging factors that have led to this market growth include frequency of travel since the 2020 pandemic and the rise of RV manufacturers in the U.S. and Canada.

Target Market

The target market for Ben's RV Rentals are mostly travelers in their late 20s with families with two or more children, as well as families with pets who want to take their pets along with them wherever they travel.

Competitive Advantage

Most of the competitors in the region do provide RV rental services. Ben's RV Rentals will stand out by providing newer RVs, such as electric RVs and multi-amenity RVs which cater to the various lifestyles of different customers.

Barriers and Regulations

There are fewer barriers of entry to get into the RV rental market, but there are some regulations to follow, such as XXX, XXX, and XXX.

Products and Services

The next section of your business plan should explain the products and services you are selling. This is where you will share how your offer benefits the customers and solves their problems. Additionally, this is the section where you can share plans for applying for intellectual property rights, such as copyrights, or patents for the products or services you sell, if applicable.

This section in your business plan is absolutely essential because this is the main driver of operations for what's being built at the core of your business. Potential investors, lenders, employees, and other stakeholders should have some insight into what you are selling to see the revenue potential it has.

Things to Include in the Products and Services Section

As this section outlines what your business offers to your customers, you will need to include the following:

- a list of your product line or services you offer
- a detailed explanation of each product and/or service and how they can solve the target customer's problem
- the pricing model for your products and services to give a good idea of how you will price your offerings and give better clarity of your revenue potential

- your ideal target customers you are looking to offer your products and services to
- your potential sales and distribution strategy and how your supply chain management will ensure you fulfill each order
- any additional information, such as an outline of potential patents, trademarks, and copyrights linked with your product or service

Writing a Good Products and Services Section

I would say this section is probably what readers look forward to the most because seeing a list of products and services often entices them, and this can be something you can take good advantage of. Here are a few pointers you can keep in mind while writing this section:

Define the Need for Your Product or Service

Fundamentally, you will need to indicate the reasons for why your products and services are required in the market. This is where you will reference the problem statement once again, list the target customer's pain points, and introduce how your product or service will fix them. It is all about convincing your readers that your product or service is absolutely the answer.

Address the Features

Another important detail, which many fail to include, would be each product's or service's features. This is where you can separate yourself and stand out against other businesses who are offering similar products and services to yours. Be sure to focus on the different features, the pricing, and the unique advantages of using your product or service.

Don't Forget the Benefits

Alongside the importance of describing features, I want to stress that benefits are even more vital, as this is all about providing value to your customers. Your features can be translated into benefits, and this will convince your readers that you know what you are offering and how much customers will look forward to buying your product. For instance, a feature such as a chair with ergonomic capabilities can be translated into providing customers with comfort that also helps them avoid injuries while sitting for a long time at work.

Always Be Straight to the Point

Ensure that you are being clear and concise with your writing, and don't include too many irrelevant product details or service descriptions that can cause your reader to lose interest. Just like what was explained earlier in the Executive Summary section, you will need to make your copy concise and scannable so that readers who are quickly reading through it can easily comprehend your list of products and services.

Bring Up Your Credentials

After describing all of your products and services, you will then need to convince your readers why you are the right person to provide them. This is where you can prop up your business background by writing about your education, experience in the industry, and any accolades that make you an expert in this field. This is all about showing that you have the product or service knowledge and that you know what you are talking about.

It Is All About Your Customers

43

Always remember that this section should be centered around your target customers, so you should focus on how you will solve their problems. You can always show off how special your products and services are, but this should always be aligned with solving the customer's problems and showing your readers that you truly care about providing value in the market.

Example of a Products and Services Section

Here is another brief example of a Products and Services section. You can follow this format or use paragraphs to add more description for each product or service you offer.

Eneco Woodworking Shop Inc.

Summary

Eneco Woodworking Shop sells woodworking tools and machinery to individual woodworkers and woodworking businesses that require essential tools to support them in woodworking projects.

Product List

Our product line currently includes the following:

For small workshops and individuals, we offer pocket-size woodworking machinery in bulk, such as:

- circular saw
- miter saw
- table saw
- impact driver
- drill machine

For larger workshops, industries, and woodworking corporations, we provide industrial woodworking machinery in bulk, such as:

- table saw
- band saw
- drill press
- jointer
- planer
- router
- wood crushers
- wood panel maker
- wood lathe

Target Customers

Our target customers will prefer products based on their projects and how large their workshops are, but the aforementioned are our predefined products that will target specific individuals and companies with the best woodworking tool profiles.

Distribution Strategy

Our plan is to source these woodworking tools from suppliers our owners have connections with, and also from ecommerce websites such as Ali Express and from wholesale in bulk. We will store the inventory in our warehouse and use our logistical partners to deliver woodworking machinery to our clients in need of equipment.

Pricing List

Eneco Woodworking Shop Inc. also offers products at the following price points:

- table saw: $XX
- circular saw: $XX
- miter saw: $XX
- impact driver: $XX
- drill machine: $XX
- band saw: $XX
- drill press: $XX
- jointer: $XX
- planer: $XX
- router: $XX
- wood crushers: $XX
- wood panel maker: $XX
- wood lathe: $XX

Since this example is about a woodworking company that sources machinery and tools from other suppliers, it wouldn't be necessary to include anything about intellectual property, such as patents.

Marketing and Sales Plan

In the marketing and sales section, this is where you will explain how you will win customers and retain them. You will go through how you are going to make sales and talk about the different marketing strategies you will implement to strengthen your brand and generate more qualified leads. Delivering customer satisfaction is important to establish loyalty so that you can keep customers coming back and create a profitable long-term business.

This portion of your business plan is important because it is one of the key indicators for how you plan to generate profits and develop exposure to sell your products and services. Let's be real! You can have the best product or service in the world, but if no one can find you or has even heard of you, it won't matter at all. You need to focus on marketing and sales strategies in order to get your offer in front of the interested customers and close every deal possible.

Developing marketing and sales tactics is crucial because you need to show your potential investors and stakeholders that you are fully prepared to do all it takes to bring revenue through your business door. This is a good thing to show to whomever is reading your business plan, so be fully confident and put faith in your project; show that you know how to expose your solution to your target market.

How to Write Your Marketing and Sales Plan

There is nothing complicated about writing a good marketing and sales plan. Your section should contain the following pieces of information so that you touch upon all the essential points required. They are as follows:

Value Proposition

So, your value proposition is basically the problem you are trying to solve in the market. This is where you will present a unique value proposition that plays like a special ingredient that you have and other competitors don't. Your value proposition doesn't need to be one thing. It might be a combination of things, such as delivering excellent customer service, utilizing advanced technology to solve the problem, or extra features that solve multiple problems for the customer. This is where you will deliver your pitch for your product or service and why you think it will bring revenue to your company.

Pricing

The next inclusion should be about your pricing strategy. One good tip for setting your prices is to first analyze the prices of your competition. This will give you a good idea of how much their customers are willing to spend, and hence, you know you can charge similar prices. It is all about setting an economical price that satisfies the customers and also brings marginal gains to your business. Price cutting is one way to stand out against other competitors, and this is done by charging very low prices, but eventually, customers will prefer to go for quality products and services. Price cutting can harm your business operational costs and could lead to low profit margins.

Sales and Distribution

When it comes to getting your products and services to your customers, you will need to plan that effectively. This is where you will outline your sales and distribution strategies to show your readers how you will get your offer to the doorstep of your consumers. It can include strategies such as direct selling, door-to-door sales, etc. When it comes to your distribution, you will need to think about whether your company will have retail stores, carry out transactions virtually, or use other means to deliver the products or services to your customers.

Marketing

Next up, you will need to include an in-depth pitch regarding your marketing plan. This is where you will include information on how you plan to win customers. You can utilize marketing strategies such as digital marketing, advertising, word-of-mouth, referrals, public relations, etc. Marketing is a long-term game. It is all about planning strategies to keep attracting customers and developing a brand name. Utilizing design elements and getting visual images of your brand in front of your customers will often increase the chances of your business being exposed to large groups of people in your target market. For planning this section efficiently, utilize the 5 'P's of Marketing:

- **Product**: The product/service you are offering to customers. This includes its features, appearance, branding, packaging, and quality.
- **Place**: Where and when your products reach your customers. This includes logistics, distribution channels, and market reach.
- **Price**: The price of each product or service you will set. This includes pricing strategy, cost of goods, markup price, offers, and discounts.
- **Promotion**: Talk about ways in which you will be promoting your products and services. This includes devising marketing strategies like advertising, social media marketing, SEO, public relations, etc.
- **People**: These are the people involved in your entire process. This includes your employees, customers, suppliers, and partners.

Budget

After stating all your marketing and sales initiatives, you will need to include some financial estimations for all these activities. You will need to calculate how much you are willing to invest in each marketing initiative and how much you will need from investors who decide to get onboard. You should put these estimations in a clean and professional format. You might state that you expect to get 100-200 clients through carrying out digital marketing by investing XX amount of dollars in social media, XX amount of dollars in video marketing, another XX amount in email marketing, etc. Most importantly, it is crucial to plan ahead, as this will be useful when laying out the plans for your financial section of your business plan.

Conducting Research for Your Sales and Marketing Plan

In order to prepare your Marketing and Sales plan, it is crucial to do some research beforehand so you can develop effective marketing and sales strategies that will stand out against your competitors and attract more customers.

You might choose to follow one or both of the following research techniques, which involve two methods:

Qualitative: Research that focuses on quality of responses. It has more to do with how and why. This information is basically determined through emotions and opinions.

Quantitative: Research that focuses on the quantity of the responses. It has more to do with how much or how many. This information is basically determined through numbers.

Here are a few ways you can conduct research to learn more about your target market:

- interviews with target customers
- focus groups
- observation studies
- pricing research studies
- product/service testing

You can find a lot of information on the internet or conduct these studies yourself with assistance.

Another important research method you can use for your marketing purposes involves studying the macroeconomic trends (external factors) that affect your organization. This is known as the PESTEL Analysis. The abbreviation stands for:

- **Political**: Factors that are driven by actions and policies set by the government.

Example: tax, trade disputes, regulations, etc.

- **Economic**: Factors that relate to the economy as a whole and affect the financial system.

Example: inflation, interest rates, exchange rates, etc.

- **Social**: Factors that are societal in nature and affect the economical trends and behavior.

Example: consumer lifestyle trends, beliefs, attitudes, demographics, etc.

- **Technological**: Factors that are technological and affect the market economy as we know it.

Example: cyber security, infrastructure, internet, etc.

- **Environmental**: Factors that belong to our physical environment that can present opportunities or risks in the market.

Example: natural resources, natural disasters, climate change, etc.

- **Legal**: Factors that belong to the regulatory environment that play a role in affecting the economy.

Example: intellectual property rights, consumer protection laws, licenses, regulations, etc.

Example of a Sales and Marketing Plan

Here is a brief example of a sales and marketing plan which touches upon the objective, strategies, tactics, and distribution plans for acquiring target customers.

Media Digital Zone

Value Proposition

To offer digital marketing services to cosmetic doctors in order for them to get exposure online and win more clients/patients. The goal is to close at least two cosmetic doctors per month in the first year and offer them our digital marketing services.

Marketing Plan

Target Customer

- Professional cosmetic doctors who are based in home clinics or own their cosmetic clinics.
- Cosmetic doctors who are living within a 10-mile radius of our agency.
- Ideal target customers would be cosmetic doctors who are busy all day and have no time to carry out marketing initiatives.
- They are also active on social media.

Marketing Strategies

- Connect with hospitals and clinics nearby to find contacts for cosmetic doctors in need of marketing services.
- Offer a 1-month trial package to cosmetic doctors to help them decide if they are happy with the service and offer upgrades later.
- Offer subscription services later on, with a XX% discount to get them onboard for a long-term business relationship.

Marketing Tactics

- Run social media marketing ads on Facebook, LinkedIn, and Pinterest—target cosmetic doctors within the 10-mile radius.
- Utilize aggressive email marketing with persuasive copy to prospects and implement at least 5 follow-up emails until they eventually agree to a discovery call.
- Example of an email—Are you spending all of your budget on marketing while we can bring in about XX% ROI in just 6 months?

Marketing Frequency

- Run social media marketing ads on Facebook, LinkedIn, and Pinterest at different times during the week and day to evaluate the ideal response rate.
- Send emails at least 5 times a week to new prospects, with a follow-up email being sent to each prospect once a week.

- Produce content for blog at least 3 times per month to increase awareness of the company for cosmetic doctors.

Performance Measurement

- number of clicks
- number of emails opened/click rate
- number of times prospect visits the landing page
- number of contacts made in social media
- number of discovery calls booked
- number of clients onboarded through each marketing channel
- cost for acquiring each new client, including the time it took
- retention rate %

Budget

We are going to allot at least $XXX to covering our marketing expenses and ensuring all campaigns run smoothly according to our schedule.

Financial Plan

You can't simply work on your marketing and sales section of your business plan if you are ignoring the financial side of things. As a startup, it is crucial that you estimate some finances, even if you don't have much information yet regarding your business's financial requirements.

If you are an established business, you will need to include your typical profit-loss statements, a balance sheet, and cash flow statements to present an analysis of the financial performance of your business. A profit-loss statement helps to determine whether your business has seen a profit or loss in recent years. The balance sheet determines what assets and liabilities the business has owned or owed throughout the years. And a cash flow statement tells investors whether you are seeing more cash inflow in your business or mostly cash outflow. It is clear that you need to show how much money is coming in and how much is going out. And most importantly, how much profit are you making?

Making Financial Projections

You may be wondering how you can approach this section of the business plan. Providing a financial presentation is important, but how do you do it if you are just a startup? Don't worry. This part will come to you naturally after you have completed extensive research on your market analysis, products and services, marketing and sales plan, etc. This is why the financial plan is usually written toward the end of the business plan.

You can provide a financial plan for, let's say, the first five years with projected income statements, cash flow statements, balance sheets, and a budget expenditure plan. You can use specific figures and make forecasts. Ensure all these projections match up with your funding requests. Utilizing charts and graphical representations can be helpful for your readers to scan through your section efficiently, and this type of presentation can tell a good financial story about your company.

You can estimate your financial projections roughly, since you are going to start a business, by following these steps:

- Estimate your expenses.

- Estimate your sales.
- Craft financial projections and prepare a profit and loss statement.
- Assess and determine your financial needs.
- Use the projections for planning.
- Monitor the trends by using charts and graphs.

For enhancing the credibility of this section even further, you can make use of different metrics, such as calculating the net profit margin (a percentage of revenue you keep as profit), current ratio (number of assets that can meet the number of liabilities you have), turnover ratio (cost of goods sold divided by average inventory), etc.

Example of a Financial Plan

Here is a brief example template of a financial plan that you can use to find inspiration when writing your business plan.

Bullish Investment Co.

Forecast Plan

Forecasted Revenue by Month (for the first year): insert graph or chart

Forecasted Expenses by Month (for the first year): insert graph or chart

Forecasted Profit or Loss by Year (for the first 3-5 years): insert graph or chart

Assumptions made during the forecast:

- Constant regulatory environment
- Stable investment market

- Rise of social media lead generation and enhanced digital marketing tools
- Usage of well-defined metrics to measure performance levels and capture results

Financing Plan

Usage of Funds

When it comes to usage of funds, Bullish Investment Co. will invest in the following costs for its startup (these are considered to be assets):

- Office space and rent
- Workspace desks, chairs, and other office furniture
- Office supplies like pens, paper, etc.
- Hardware such as printers, computers, fax machines, scanners, etc.
- Legal costs for forming the business and trade registration

Source of Funds

One of Bullish Investment Co.'s partners, Mr. A, will incur all these costs.

Financial Statements

In this section, we have prepared projected financial statements.

Projected P&L Account: insert table

Projected Balance Sheet: insert table

Projected Cash Flow Statement: insert table

As the above statements show, Bullish Investment Co. is planning to make around $XXX profit within the first three years of its business formation.

Funding Request

This section is optional and reserved for plans in which you will need to ask for funding. If you are planning to request funding, you will need to outline in detail what your funding requirements are. It is important to be articulate and straightforward rather than beating around the bush or asking in a shy manner. You need to tell your reader clearly that you want the necessary funding for the first three to five years of your upstart. This request comes after they have gone through your product/service list, management style, marketing and sales plan, and your financial projections.

Writing a Clear Funding Request Page

To craft an effective Funding Request section of your business plan, look to include the following details:

- Clearly explain what you will use the funds for and how you will use them.
- Write it in a clear and concise manner. Do not use repetitive words and redundant information.
- Decide if you want debt or equity.
- Specify the time period which your funding request will cover.
- Be transparent when you list out all the things you will use the funds for. For instance, you can write down that you will use it to buy furniture and equipment, pay salaries to employees and vendors, pay utility bills, etc.

- Include a brief description of your future financial plans, such as how much funding you would need in the future for expansion, etc.

Example of a Funding Request

Here is an example of a funding request, which is written briefly. Feel free to utilize headers and group your funding request requirements neatly to make the page more readable for your potential investors and lenders.

Darwin Office Solutions Inc.

Company Overview and Value Proposition

Darwin Office Solutions Inc. is an office furniture supplier that provides office solutions for small businesses. We also offer a wide range of hardware solutions along with our office solutions with one of our co-owners, Mr. A, who has several connections with IT companies because of his experience in this industry.

Usage of Funds

The following are our financial requirements for starting up our business, as well as what it will be used for:

- Registration and Legal $XX
- Insurance expenses $XX
- Office Rent $XX
- Office Equipment and Supplies $XX
- Warehouse Costs $XX
- Marketing materials $XX
- Other startup costs $XX

Richard Hedberg

Total Funding Requirement = $XXXX

Source of Funds

After going through the table, it is estimated that we would require an initial funding of $XXX to carry our business operations and attain profitability in the first few years. We can meet these financial requirements through bank loans, equipment leases, and other investments. We are looking for a startup capital loan of around $XX.

Future Plan

We are seeking to sustain a minimum of XX% gross margins after the first year of company formation. We are planning to improve our inventory management, which in turn will improve our business operations. As a result, this will increase our net sales by XX% after three years.

Appendix

The final section of the business plan is your Appendix, where you can include any additional information or supporting materials that may be requested by your potential stakeholders. This section should include information that is important but that didn't fit in any of the preceding sections. You will know as you move through your plan what information would be more logically fitting toward the end. Make sure you include the Appendix as a title when making your Table of Contents page at the beginning of your business plan.

Here are some examples of things that might be included in your Appendix:

- resumes
- licenses and certifications
- leases
- permits
- bank statements
- contracts
- intellectual property rights, like patents, trademarks, and copyrights
- credit histories
- photographs of your products
- letters of reference
- other associated legal documents

You have now learned all about the fundamental elements you will need to include in a typical business plan. You are free to modify the content in any way you want, but keep in mind that you are doing this to sell your pitch to important readers who may make or break your startup, so think from their perspective in addition to your own. Each section in this chapter has provided a brief example from which you can gain inspiration and customize.

You can utilize the templates, but make sure your sections are written in order and that all are included in your business plan. For the Executive Summary, feel free to write it toward the end, as mentioned earlier, but it is usually best to write it first and then revisit it later to revise and include any improvements. Treat each section seriously, and put your passion in your writing so that your readers will feel the same about it.

We have talked a great deal about your readers. The next chapter will explore how you can win customers early on in your business.

Key Takeaways From This Chapter

- Your business plan consists of the following elements when you write it—Executive Summary, Company Description, Market Analysis, Products and Services, Marketing and Sales Plan, Financial Plan and Projections, Funding Request, and Appendix.
- Your Executive Summary is a brief one- or two-page summary of your company that states the goal, mission, company overview, products, services, marketing, and financial analysis, written concisely.
- Your Company Description is the information about your company's background that lists the names of owners, the business legal structure, management style, business location, etc.
- The Market Analysis is the market research you conduct in your industry by evaluating the target market demands, competitors, and other regulating factors.
- Your Products and Services section should list all your offerings: what they are, how they will solve your target market problems, and how much they will be priced for.
- Your Sales and Marketing Plan should consist of marketing and sales strategies and tactics that you will use to win customers and retain them for your business.
- Your Financial Plan should consist of financial analyses, fund allocation, source of funds, and financial projections of your business, potentially

using statements such as Profit and Loss statement, Cash Flow statement, and Balance Sheet.

- Your Funding Request page should consist of all the information you will provide to potential investors or lenders regarding how much in funding will be required to start business operations, including how you will use the money and any future fund requirements for growth and expansion plans.
- The last section is your Appendix, where you will add supporting documents and materials that don't fit in other sections of your business plan but are still important to your potential readers. This might include resumes, contracts, intellectual property rights, photographs, etc.

Chapter 3

Building Relationships with Customers

Wonder what your customer really wants? Ask. Don't tell.

— Lisa Stone

T he previous chapter was all about writing your business plan in an organized manner. You should now understand how to write one and how to include the most important information in each section. Once you have prepared a business plan, you will need to commit to your promises. All those forecasted financial analyses, marketing and sales plans, and funding requests shouldn't go to waste, especially when you have successfully received the funds you needed to start your business operations (in which case, congratulations!). You will need to back up all your work by attaining profits. How can you do that? By increasing revenue. And how can you do that? *Customers.* You need customers.

To this end, this chapter will discuss how you can build and maintain relationships with your customers because this is so important for the success of your business. If you can get customers who are loyal to you for the lifetime of your business, you are going to increase your revenue and maintain a healthy rate of growth for your business.

Maintaining relationships with your current clients and building lifetime value for those who remain loyal will help ease the pressure to spend lots of money on aggressive marketing initiatives. You want to be in the preferable position of taking care of the loyal customer base you have rather than having to always look for ways to get new ones in the door. If you are in for the long-term, you definitely need to keep your clients close and maintain relationships with them. You need to deliver service that maintains consistent customer satisfaction so that they continue to refer new clients to you and won't switch over to your competitors.

Let us dive further into this topic and discuss how you can grow your customer base, connect with your customers during the digital age, and, most importantly, build customer loyalty and maintain a healthy relationship with them.

Growing Your Customer Base

Whether you are a startup or an established business, you need customers consistently coming to you. Whether they are new or old, your customer base must grow so that you are bringing in revenue and mitigating any risk of going out of business. Here are a few strategies you can use to attract new customers and grow your customer base.

Run Ads

This is the most traditional method of capturing your target customer's attention. Advertisement is appealing, and it does the job of communicating a message to your target audience about their specific problem and introduces them to the solution—your product or service. Traditional advertising methods such as having ads in magazines, newspapers, or billboards still work, but digital marketing initiatives such as ads on social media like LinkedIn, Facebook, Instagram, and Pinterest are even stronger nowadays. As the world is more online and consumers are glued to their smartphones, it is easier to reach your target customers by running ad campaigns online using various forums, platforms, email marketing, and social media, in particular.

Referrals

This is one of the most overlooked techniques, especially when there is a lot of competition and uncertainty in the market. When someone refers your business to their friends, colleagues, or any other connection they have, this cuts down on your need for marketing initiative expenditures and spreads your message via word of mouth. You will find yourself sitting back and relaxing while your current clients spread the word about you and bring in new clients to you. You need to convince your customers to refer their connections to you. You can do this by getting them to think about someone they know who is similar in persona and require similar products or services as you are providing them. This usually sparks at least one person in their minds, and then their referral can provide you with a potential lead. Can you imagine the possibilities if one of your clients had a huge pool of strong connections, and they ended up getting all of them to sign up with you? You'd be bringing in exponential leads based on that single referral alone. This is how amazing asking for referrals can be. You can build a referral system in your sales process by sending follow-up emails asking for referrals, or by starting a referral program where your current clients are offered incentives for bringing in good leads to your business.

Network

This is a traditional way of acquiring customers, regardless of whatever business you are in. When you spread the word about your business and connect with lots of people and organizations relevant to your industry, you are building a network. You can attend networking events and meet people that way, or you can reach out to people by joining social media networking sites such as LinkedIn. Always remember that you shouldn't present as desperate to sell your products and services to anyone you meet for the first time. Connect by offering assistance and getting to know people in the industry rather than placing the emphasis on yourself and getting your own business ahead. You will be amazed at the relationships you can build when you focus on providing value to people first. They will begin to perceive you as a reliable person and come to you for business. Moreover, they will have you in mind when they have associates who are in need of your business's service or products, which is a big plus.

Offer Incentives

When it comes to acquiring new customers, try offering incentives, such as a good one-time offer for new customers that will help them see the value in signing up for your products or services. This can be pretty risky sometimes, as you are sacrificing some portion of your profit margin to win new customers who may or may not stick with you, but this strategy can help you in the long-term, especially if you sign high-paying and loyal customers who will offset the cost of your initial offer. In the end, it is all about exciting your new customers and making them an offer that is very difficult to refuse.

Old Customers

Sometimes, it is easy to get new business if you come back to your old customers again. It may sound unproductive at first, but if you have already done business with someone and they liked your service, why not ask them again if they need your product or service? You can approach this by going through your old client database and contacting them to check in and remind them that your business is available. For example, ask an old client how their business has been going and how their previous business experience with you has benefitted their organization. Then, you can ask them if they require anything currently. If they do, that's great! If they don't, ask for referrals, and you should at least get one good lead from doing that. If you have made your old clients happy before, oftentimes they will be glad to do you a little favor even if they don't have a current need.

Update Your Website

Whether you have an ecommerce business or a physical business, your website is often the main attraction and first impression for your business. Nowadays, almost every business will have a website that displays all the important information, such as their company overview, staff, and a list of products and services they provide. Therefore, take your website seriously by hiring a web designer who can make sure your site is accessible, friendly, and easy to comprehend and navigate for prospective customers visiting for the first time.

Ensure that you have an SEO-friendly (Search Engine Optimized) website so that your business will be ranked higher up on search engines like Google. SEO works best when you follow a set of guidelines. These guidelines include the following:

- Utilize the most-searched keywords that your target customers enter frequently on search engines by including them in your website copy, blogs, and other marketing content—Google or other search engines will use the magic of the search engine algorithm to expose your website via your target market's search results.
- Avoid overstuffing of keywords, especially within close proximity of one another.
- Add internal and external links to your content. Internal links are links that take you to content on your own website. Whereas external links are links that take you away from your website and to a credible source on someone else's website. Including both will improve the authority of your website, which is helpful for Google's algorithm, and the search engine will promote the website to be higher up in the search results pages.

Partner

Another good way of getting new customers is to partner with local and international businesses that have a similar target market. For instance, if you are an ERP software provider, you can partner with hardware solutions stores and other IT companies and get access to their customer base in exchange for a commission for referrals and using their products for your advantage. The world of business is a free world, and you can use these tactics—while respecting all the laws—to ensure you get access to as many prospects as possible.

Online Testimonials and Reviews

There is something peculiar about humans, which is that we are social creatures who judge most things based heavily on social factors. If we see a restaurant that is empty, we will probably perceive it as a poor restaurant and avoid going there. On the other hand, if we see another restaurant nearby packed with people, we will probably perceive it as a good restaurant and be more likely to enter there. Likewise, this applies to how you can get customers for your business. Win positive online reviews and testimonials to increase your chances of getting more leads and convincing new customers to do business with you by delivering a top-notch product or service.

Participate

Taking part in community events helps to raise your business's profile and build some reputation. This will help you win customers, sponsors, and partners to help you grow your business. You must have the participative mindset to give something back to the community, and you will soon see the benefits as time goes by. On top of that, this is a great opportunity to entice people by introducing your expertise in your particular industry. You can do this by participating in online or offline webinars, toastmasters, and other productive events that can help you get your and your business's name to your audience's ears.

Connecting with Customers

Connecting with your customers is crucial to increase engagement and your chances of converting them into long-term clients. Interaction is necessary, and nothing can be automated completely in this regard using AI (Artificial Intelligence). You need that human element in there to fully understand your customer requirements and connect with them through empathy.

Here are a few tips you can keep in mind to improve your chances of connecting better with customers.

Everyone's Different

The biggest mistake one can make is to approach each customer thinking that all their requirements are the same and that they have the same tastes. One size of a shoe won't fit everyone. Similarly, you will need to approach each as an individual and look for ways their needs can be met by you as a supplier.

Listen More Than You Talk

We are all guilty of doing this sometimes as someone who is selling their product or service. We tend to speak more than we listen because we desperately want to close that sale. However, this causes a negative impression on the customer, who might feel they are not being heard or only being dominated by the seller. Ensure you listen more so you can understand their requirements clearly.

Implement the art of mirroring by repeating back some of the words they say regarding their requirements, as this assures them that you are a good listener and ready to help them rather than just being a pushy salesman.

71

Address Any Concerns

To connect better with your customers, make sure you are not there for business alone. You will want to earn their trust and respect by being more committed to addressing their concerns. It is all about providing the best customer experience possible.

For instance, if you are managing a food delivery app and find that a customer has suffered a bad experience and lost money in their last purchase, you must look to contact the customer directly and listen to their concerns. Moreover, offer them a coupon to express your deepest apologies for the technical issue your app has caused them.

The Art of Follow-Up

When it comes to being persistent and earning customer appreciation, following up on a regular basis can be an effective strategy, as long as you are respecting their privacy. Following up helps to remind them of you, despite how busy their day has been.

This will also help you to earn trust and respect, letting your customers know that you are there for more than just doing business. Your customers like to feel that they are being noticed and provided with hospitality, so following up should be part of your system.

Add a Human Touch to Things

Remember that your interactions shouldn't always be kept transactional, too formal, or robotic when dealing with your customers. They are human, after all, just like you. Ensure that you are more personal with your customers—while respecting their privacy—so that you get to strengthen the connection and learn more about their needs.

Face-to-Face Does Wonders

I know it is the digital era and everyone is connecting with prospects online through social media, video conferences, etc. Moreover, reaching them through emails and phone calls can do good things, too. But there is something much more effective about meeting your client face-to-face. You will increase the chances of connecting with them more deeply, and they will feel more comfortable expressing their needs clearly to you.

I know this can be difficult, especially if you are reaching out to clients on a global scale, but if you are reaching out to clients locally, you will have a better chance of increasing your customers' lifetime value if you go have a face-to-face conversation and establish a personal business relationship.

Be Alert on Social Media

Most businesses these days generate leads using the power of social media. You will benefit massively from having a social media account on each major platform, including Facebook, LinkedIn, Instagram, TikTok, and Pinterest. Establishing an online presence in social media is a great way to connect with your customers. You should be sharing content on social media regularly, engaging with prospects' comments, and answering their queries. Customers keep talking about different brands on social media, and the digital word-of-mouth can be powerful in reaching millions of prospective customers if your company name is mentioned.

Keep Up with Your Current Clients

Your business will keep growing toward greater heights if you are consistent in delivering customer satisfaction and keep them happy. It can be overwhelming as an entrepreneur to be engaged with many other things, and you may end up forgetting to pay attention to all your clients. That's why most top companies have a specific system in their customer relationship process, where after signing up a new client, they receive a follow-up email or visit in the first week and another one within the first few months. It is all about giving attention and appreciation to show them that you are reliable and there for them no matter what.

Do the Research

Regardless of how well you do on the customer service side of things, there is still a lot to learn—especially with how unpredictable the market can be. One excellent way to stay up to date is to conduct surveys to learn more about your customers' needs and wants. This will help you to understand your customers better and gain valuable feedback regarding concerns which you may not have thought of in the first place. Their input is crucial, and this can help you not only connect better with them but also craft a solution that caters to every requirement they have.

Building Customer Loyalty

Your business's revenue potential and reputation is built around how much value you can deliver to your customers. To maintain a sustainable and profitable business, you need to have a secured customer base that consists of repeat buyers who keep coming back to you, as well as new clients who want a taste of what you're offering.

You must make them happy at any cost, and this will increase your chances for customer retention and satisfaction. A healthy business thrives on good customer retention because it prevents them from switching to competitors, and businesses can expect a steady profit every month from the same set of customers.

In the last section, we talked about how well you can connect with your customers. This section will give you a few pointers on how you can build customer loyalty and maintain a great relationship for a long time.

Deliver, Deliver, and Deliver

Once again, you have to bring a positive customer experience to every interaction with them, so you must consistently deliver value and address their needs. You must treat customers with respect and provide a great service. There should never be any prejudice shown, and every individual customer should have their concerns addressed. If you treat your customers like a family member, this makes your job easier, and you will be able to pay attention to the details to make their lives better. Just like we learned about value earlier in this book, your job is to take customers from their original state to a transformed state, which is the better version of themselves.

Sometimes, Get Personal

When you talk to customers on a personal level and remember important details, like their birthday or their favorite movies, this can make the customer feel appreciated and valued in your organization. We all get used to companies feeling robotic in their addressing the needs of customers. But if you want to keep your customers close to you, you can get personal sometimes and connect with them on a personal level to liven things up. Doing this will often create a positive interaction and impression, but of course, you must never overdo this part and always respect their private lives.

Don't Let the Connection Go

It is important to not abandon your customers and forget about them. They can feel this way even if you don't realize it, and this is why some companies fail to retain customers: because customers feel it when they are being ignored and left out in the communication loop. So, the lesson here is to always keep your customers in the loop and send them communications such as email newsletters, invitations to events, and an occasional follow-up email asking about any concerns that can be addressed. It is time to get more involved in the customer's world, and you can do that by keeping the connection strong with them and not isolating them.

Reward Them

Implement reward systems in your customer relationships management process by offering reward schemes or loyalty programs. This can encourage your customers to be more involved with your business and can help them feel appreci- ated, as they get their chance to dip into some pretty cool offers. In addition, this will help your business stand out against other competitors who may not be offering the same schemes, so your customers will stay with you longer and be more loyal.

Nurture the Community

When you get more involved in the community, it helps you retain your customers and build a strong and unbreakable reputation. Instead of being focused on taking, look to give more to the community by offering exclusive content and bargains. When you offer tempting deals and materials, this can entice the community to notice the value you are offering them.

Keep Appreciating Your Customers

For those customers who have been with you for a while and are bringing you good business, look to celebrate with them by inviting them to events, offering special discounts and coupons, or offering them a new test product or service for free during its initial stages. This can also increase your chances of building customer loyalty and improving retention because you are providing exclusive experiences for them.

Small Actions Lead to Greater Customer Retention

Always remember, it is those little things, such as greeting with a smile, being firm with your body language, and offering a gift that can make a big difference in how well you maintain a healthy relationship with your customers. If you want to keep winning loyal customers, it is all up to you. You start the ball rolling by delivering value, and keep them close to you by following the tips mentioned above and showing why they should stay with you.

Remember to keep appreciating your customers, address their needs for who they are, and deliver tremendous and consistent value to them. Once you build a loyal base of high-paying customers, you are definitely on track to see a steady and profitable business that will run for decades.

Customer Relationship Management

We will close this chapter by learning about customer relationship management, or in short, CRM. It is important to know this because you will be using it in your business to focus on providing customer satisfaction and retention. Customer relationship management simply refers to a set of principles and practices that a business or organization sticks to when they interact with their customers.

It is basically a system any organization should implement as part of their DNA whenever they start that first interaction with each individual customer. It basically includes all your direct and indirect interactions with customers, your marketing and sales initiatives, and the research and analysis of customer buying habits and trends. To keep things working smoothly and to introduce automation, CRM will play a major role.

Importance of CRM

CRM helps organizations to organize all their customer information and details, compiling it in one place so they can access it whenever they need to. It provides simplification and enhances work efficiency for businesses. To optimize all your marketing and sales efforts while improving your customer retention initiatives, CRM offers solutions by providing a systematic approach using software-based programs.

Back in the day, when there were no computers, businesses had to track all their customer info and various projects using pens, paper, and giant filing cabinets. It was simply too hard and quite a hassle. However, with CRMs, businesses can easily track all their projects and customer interactions by retrieving customer information quickly and prioritizing each stage of the customer journey cycle.

Technology will assist us with these things so businesses can focus all their energy on keeping their customers satisfied.

Types of CRM Solutions

Today, we have CRM software that will simplify customer information and grant businesses easy access to retrieve it anytime. We have cloud solutions that provide robust storage systems and real-time data for businesses to efficiently track projects and work on enhancing customer experience. More-over, Artificial Intelligence is now getting integrated with CRM to help make the CRM system more efficient and effective.

Here are a few types of CRMs that are designed to cater to specific needs for businesses:

- **Marketing CRM**: This type of CRM helps to automate marketing campaigns and initiatives and track all specific details regarding email campaigns and customer segment information. It also puts forward useful statistics to measure performance.
- **Sales CRM**: This type of CRM helps to foresee sales by regulating the sales pipeline and ensuring businesses stay in touch with prospects all the way through to closing the deal.
- **Service CRM**: This type of CRM helps to support customer service with marketing and sales activities. It provides features such as tracking online chats, emails, social media activity, and mobile interactions.

- **Collaborative CRM**: This type of CRM, as the name suggests, boosts sharing of customer information and data among teams as a means to enhance work efficiency and bolster communication lines.
- **CRMs for Small Businesses**: This type of CRM is specifically designed for smaller businesses or startups that are building their early customer base. It still provides these businesses with enterprise-level CRM features despite having fewer customers to manage.

CRM is a framework that helps businesses build strong relationships with customers. This is possible by combining systems and technology to maintain engagement with customers and provide them with the best service. As someone who would be starting a new business, it is important to invest in the right technology for bolstering your relationship with customers, and CRM is something worth looking into.

We've learned all about your customers in this chapter, and now we will move on in the next chapter to talking about key resources you can use in your organization to bring success to your business.

Key Takeaways From This Chapter

- Your customers are the most important assets in your business, and they determine your revenue potential and the sustainability of your company.
- You can grow your customer base by using marketing strategies, referrals, networking, offering

incentives, talking to old customers again, partnering with other businesses, updating your website, and attending events.

- You can connect with your customers better by listening more, adding a personalized touch to your interactions and communications, being present on social media, following up, having more face-to-face meetings, and doing research through surveys.
- You can build customer loyalty and retention by consistently delivering great service, rewarding customers, appreciating them, keeping them in the loop, and giving back to the community.
- Customer relationship management (CRM) simply refers to a set of principles and practices a business or an organization sticks to when they interact with their customers.
- Nowadays, with the help of CRMs, businesses can easily track all their projects and customer interactions by retrieving customer information quickly and prioritizing each stage of the customer journey cycle.

Chapter 4

Know Your Key Resources

If you really look closely, most overnight successes took a long time.

— Steve Jobs

We have learned so far about the basics of a business model and the different types, how to write a business plan to address all your business's requirements, and how to build customer relationships and retention. What we haven't talked about yet are the key resources that will build your business as a whole and play a part in delivering value to your customers on a consistent basis. I'm talking about things such as your equipment, employees, and software, among others.

All these resources play a huge role in your business's success, and they should be attended to equally with attention and care, just like you would do with your customers. So, in this chapter, we will go through the major key resources any entrepreneur should have a handle on to build their business, why they are crucial, and how you can choose and personalize them. Let's learn more about it then, shall we?

Categories of Key Resources

Your key resources will depend on your type of business, the business model, and the industry you are in. But in most cases, companies require the following five categories of key resources, which I will explain below. When you have all five of them working well in your organization, you are forming a formidable business operating model.

Physical Resources

To create a solid value proposition, one of the major key resources that play a part are the physical resources. These are your typical physical or tangible assets that you would require and utilize in your business to deliver value to your customer. For an automobile manufacturing company, they would require plenty of physical resources for their production factory such as land, machinery, and various equipment. When these resources are in place, they will be able to seamlessly produce cars and other vehicles and deliver consistent value to their customers.

In summary, your physical resources might include the following:

- infrastructure
- machinery
- equipment
- inventory
- land
- buildings

- vehicles
- materials
- energy resources
- production plant
- distribution systems
- miscellaneous

Human Resources

Your human resources are another valuable key resource you need to nurture and manage well for any organization. With employees, you are able to run a business and deliver value to multiple clients. As an entrepreneur, you cannot expect to do everything alone; if you try, you will quickly become over-whelmed and then eventually burn out. You will hate running your business because you never utilized other people.

Therefore, you need to recruit and manage people with different skill sets that will help you to fulfill different roles in your business and keep solving your customers' problems. Moreover, having other employees besides you will help you appreciate the work more and also win appreciation from your employees as you build a formidable empire together.

For any industry, or whichever type of business you are running, having people is the most important thing, and you will see their involvement concentrated and focused in a wide variety of industries, such as hospitality, healthcare, banking, and media. Recruiting and having different minds in the organization at your disposal is important for growth and development because everyone comes from a different background and can offer different creative skill sets to improve your organization in some way or another. This is the beauty of diversity, and we should be excited to work with a diverse group of people who can use their talents in the right role in your company.

Financial Resources

Let's talk about money. It is pretty evident that your financial resources—basically, money—is going to be another important resource you require. After all, you are in this to make money. You will require money for startup capital, to pay the bills to keep your business up and running, to pay vendors, and for other business-related expenses. Having good financial management is crucial in building a sustainable business and to improve your profit margins each year.

If you want to stay ahead of your competing rivals in the industry, it is essential to learn how to manage your money efficiently when it comes to spending, managing debts, and increasing revenue streams to improve cash flow.

Here are a few areas relating to business where you will see money or your financial resources involved quite a bit:

- office expenses such as paying rent and buying office equipment and furniture
- buying heavy machinery and infrastructure
- implementing hardware and software solutions, such as ERP, project management tools, and website hosting
- paying employees for their salary, healthcare, and taxes
- insurance premiums to insure your business
- expenses relating to food, travel, and hotel accommodation for business purposes
- expenses carried out for marketing initiatives, such as ad campaigns and events

- research and development costs incurred for conducting extensive market research, surveys, and focus groups
- costs for acquiring other raw materials for business purposes
- managing logistical costs in your distribution network
- paying vendors in your supply chain network
- expenses related to registering your business, logo, business cards, brochures, and trademark

Intellectual Resources

Your physical resources involve your tangible resources and assets. Your intellectual resources, however, are your intangible resources and assets that play a part in your business. This mainly includes your intellectual property (IP), such as trademarks, logos, brand, patents, copyrights, and trade secrets. For many industries, especially in the creative sectors like design, advertising, and media, intellectual property rights are very important.

Top companies safeguard these intellectual resources religiously, and that's why big brands like Microsoft, Apple, and Adidas have spent a lot of money to build their brand image and preserve their intellectual property rights. As a result, this has played a huge role in their revenue growth and business development for decades.

Things such as your business name, logos, and brand are essential and should not be overlooked when building a large client base while you are trying to reserve market share in your industry.

Digital Resources

As we live in a digital era, where businesses leverage technology to dominate the market, it is worth talking about this category as one of your key resources when forming a profitable business. Your digital resources include your software solutions that support and enhance your business workflow. When you think about tech companies such as Apple, Google, Microsoft, or Adobe, they depend on digital resources and leverage technology to produce value propositions. As a result, they dominate the marketplace and consistently deliver value to users.

Similarly, if you are an advertising or digital marketing agency, your digital resources could include digital marketing tools and your ad campaign portfolio, which help you to deliver marketing services to clients and also enhance your business growth.

In virtually any company these days, they will require digital resources in the form of internal databases, such as CRM and inventory management software, to store and retrieve data and safeguard sensitive information regarding compliance guidelines and financial statements. The days of storing papers in filing cabinets is going away, and everyone is moving to storing all their documents in cloud storage. Hence, your digital resources are the fifth and final key resource that you should manage efficiently when you are running a business.

Significance of Identifying Key Resources

Depending on the type of key resources that go into a specific business model, making good decisions in this area can determine how productive and efficient a business is in delivering value proposition to its clients. For instance, if your value proposition is bringing convenience to your clients—for example, letting users order food through an app—your objective is to ensure a clean interface with the ability to book orders efficiently and get them delivered to customers on time. In this case, you would need to invest in key resources, such as financial and human resources, to design and develop the app and the intellectual resources to protect your app's patent rights. When you look at one specific value proposition you want to fulfill at a time, you can identify the key resources you will require.

For further understanding of key resources, here are three types of businesses you can relate to your model for identifying key resources:

Product-Centered Businesses

The first type of business is centered around the product itself. These are companies that develop products and sell them to buyers. Product development is crucial for creating something unique and convincing your target market to purchase your products consistently. When looking at a product-centered business, you will see that you need to assemble key resources for products, such as intellectual resources, for protection regarding things like copyrights and patents. Moreover, you will require human resources to manufacture and develop the product. You will also need financial resources to invest in the production and marketing of the product.

Scope-Centered Businesses

This type of business emphasizes providing value to its target market as well. Here, we're focusing on delivering the value proposition. These are your typical niche businesses that specialize in delivering value to a specific customer segment, with their own expertise and resources to deliver it consistently. For example, an IT company might provide UI/UX design services to businesses who want to develop an app. Based on this type of business, you can also identify the key resources you will need to constantly achieve that value proposition.

Infrastructure-Centered Businesses

This type of business is centered around delivering value propositions through leveraging their unique and well-established infrastructure. For example, this might be universities or telecommunication companies. Based on their value proposition, these companies can identify the key resources they will need to invest in to develop their infrastructure and keep up with current demands.

Tips for Determining Your Key Resources

It is definitely vital that you analyze and evaluate each of your key resources in your business model canvas, and then invest in those that will help you achieve your value proposition. Hence, you will need pathways or indicators to help you choose the right key resources for your business.

To start your brainstorming session for determining your key resources to meet your business model canvas and value proposition, we recommend that you ask yourself four key questions:

Question #1: What key resources are required for my value propositions?

The first question is pretty basic and involves what we've been talking about throughout this chapter. You will need to ask yourself, what key resources does your value proposition or series of value propositions require? You will then identify a list of key resources and then store them safely in your computer. Just think of what basic ingredients you will need as input to utilize and produce your desired output.

Question #2: What key resources are required by my marketing, sales, and distribution channels?

The second question expands your brainstorming session by identifying the key resources that will be required in your distribution channels. Undoubtedly, your product or service won't make revenue if you don't know how to distribute it to your target market. Your marketing, sales, and distribution channels play a major role in reaching out to your audience and delivering that value proposition. Hence, identify the key resources that will help you build effective distribution channels.

Question #3: What key resources are required to establish and maintain my customer relationships?

Another important element, which was discussed in-depth in the previous chapter, is your customer relationships. Your next question is, which key resources are needed to keep delivering value to my customers and build a strong bond with them? This can help you think of key resources that will help you stand out against other competitors.

Question #4: How do these key resources support our revenue streams?

Your fourth question is to ask how your key resources will bolster your company's revenue streams. This is where you will filter all those key resources and prioritize those that will support your revenue stream and bring you profit. Sometimes, your brainstorming sessions might build a list of too many key resources that would be a waste of time and money, without being effective for your business processes. Hence, this question is crucial to ask yourself last so that you can narrow things down to those that will contribute to your ultimate goals.

Let us apply this reasoning to another business example:

Let's imagine you are a realtor who is trying out an Airbnb business model (short-term rental business). Your value proposition is to deliver convenience to your customers when they check in to a vacation home by providing all the necessary amenities until the time that they check out. To achieve this, you know you will need to ensure their safety and provide the amenities that will satisfy the customers' needs.

You will also need to think of key resources to help you market your short-term rental home and gain exposure. Brainstorm for other unique key resources that can help you maintain customer relationships, earn good ratings on Airbnb, and encourage customers to book a stay with you again in the future.

Based on this thinking, you determine the following list of key resources that you will need:

- **Physical resources**: amenities such as bath towels, soap, toilet paper, water, refreshments, etc.; technology such as TV, security system, HVAC
- **Human resources**: cleaning crew that will clean and prep your vacation home after every turnover; repair and maintenance crew that will fix damages and replace damaged furniture

- **Financial resources**: incur cost for the above resources and initial startup cost to buy or rent a short-term rental home in a good location
- **Intellectual resources**: trademark to register and protect your business; other legal documents
- **Digital resources**: photographs of the home to upload online for Airbnb site; host a website and reach out to different prospects using various online marketing tools

Assembling Effective Key Resources for Your Business Model

It is not uncommon for many entrepreneurs to fail to plan strategically when it comes to identifying and assembling key resources to achieve their value propositions. Hence, one way to combat this is to look at other businesses first. Study the common key resources that most successful businesses use and emulate that in your own business framework. This will help you to get more than half of your job done properly, and then you can identify what further key resources will help you create more value and make your business unique from other competitors. This is probably the simplest thing you can do because we can all benefit from letting other successful businesses inspire us; talking about a lazy man's strategy, it is usually best to mimic others' good qualities if you want to compete in the market.

Another way to determine your key resources is to do a little bit of reverse engineering. Suppose you've already thought about how your value proposition will be achieved. For instance, using the above example, you've already delivered customer satisfaction by providing a pleasurable experience to those staying in your short-term rental home. Now, you will take a look at what key activities contributed to reaching that desired outcome. This list will become evident as you think of all your amenities, technology, and customer experience initiatives that went into crafting a superior experience. You should also find some feedback from those who've left you a positive review. Look at what was mentioned specifically; perhaps your clients appreciated the brand-new appliances in the kitchen, for example. Just like an architect or engineer, you can slowly start analyzing each key activity or amenity and learn how to improve upon it. As a result, you will be able to identify the key resources required for each activity and utilize the four-questions model to prioritize those resources that support your revenue and maintain good customer relationships.

As an entrepreneur, you will need to use your resources to your advantage and manage them efficiently. They will have a huge effect on your business and future plans based on how you use them. Hence, resource planning and allocation is an important skill to have as an entrepreneur who is looking to make their business successful. Utilize a prioritization model that involves delegating resources to others if this task is overwhelming for you. Utilize resources immediately to achieve an expedient value proposition, and save resources for later use if it is important but will only serve a purpose later. Finally, eliminate resources from your business that have no value or purpose for future plans.

Key Takeaways From This Chapter

- Key resources build your business as a whole and play a part in delivering value to your customers consistently.

- There are five categories of key resources: physical resources, human resources, financial resources, intellectual resources, and digital resources.
- There are three types of businesses that can help you determine the importance of key resources: product-centered businesses, scope-centered businesses, and infrastructure-centered businesses.
- Use the four-questions model to ask yourself the four key questions to determine key resources to help you achieve your value proposition, build your distribution channels, build customer relationships, and support your revenue streams.
- Assembling key resources efficiently as an entrepreneur can be a challenge. You can utilize the reverse engineering methodology by analyzing the key activities that help you achieve your value propositions.
- It is crucial to utilize and allocate your resources efficiently—especially if they are scarce and you have constraints to combat. Utilize a prioritization model and save useful resources, delegate other important resources to others, and eliminate completely resources that have no value for your business.

Chapter 5

Pitch Your Business Plan

When we do what we are meant to do, money comes to us, doors open for us, we feel useful, and the work we do feels like play to us.

— Julia Cameron

The previous two chapters should have given you a good understanding of how to run your business and back up the plan you've prepared in your draft. Coming back to business plans again, you will need to present a solid pitch to sell your plan to investors—especially if you are looking for the initial funds to start your business operation. In most cases, new entrepreneurs will need to depend on external parties to fund their businesses. But no one is going to just lend you money without being sold on your idea, especially banks.

Therefore, this chapter is going to go through how you can pitch your business plan by identifying key investors, presenting your business plan pitch strategy, and approaching different parties until you get that "yes."

Know Where Your Funding Comes From

As an entrepreneur looking to launch your new business, it can be a big challenge early on to maintain your working capital. In pure financial terms, your working capital is the balance between your current assets and liabilities of your business. If you find yourself with larger current liabilities than your current assets, then that spells trouble concerning your working capital. You always want your current assets to exceed your current liabilities in order to meet your daily business operation expenses.

As you prepare your business plan, you will need to decide who you are going to request your funds from. For that, you will need to fully understand where it all comes from. Here are a few sources from which you can acquire your funds for that initial working capital and beyond to meet your daily business operational needs.

Loans

Without a shadow of a doubt, one of the most common ways of getting a new business up and running is seeking a business loan from financial institutions. A business loan typically is an agreement formed between the lender (usually a bank or any other financial institution) and the business owner—which is you. The lender will provide you with a fixed amount of money you require, and you have to pay it back with interest within a fixed repayment period. Nowadays, you will find business loans which are catered to allow flexibility for business owners, providing them with more choices for setting predefined criteria.

Despite its big advantage of instantly solving the business owner's financial needs, there are some things you need to keep in mind. In order to get a business loan approved, you must maintain a high credit rating and history. Moreover, you could be subjected to high interest rates per annum depending on the bank or institution you deal with and also based on your credit score.

Business Line of Credit

The business line of credit is basically a flexible loan provided to businesses that also acts as a credit card. You will be given a credit line, and you can take out money to use for your business operations. So, essentially, it acts like a revolving loan that you can get from banks and certain financial institutions to meet your working capital requirements from time to time.

You are allowed to use the capital to meet your business requirements and repay the loan immediately or within a specified time period. Indeed, an interest rate is also applied, just like a regular loan. The only difference between a business credit line and a regular business loan is that you get more flexibility to take out and pay back the money with a business credit line, whereas with a regular loan, the amount and repayment period are fixed.

Similar to business loans, your approval for getting a business line of credit also depends on your credit score and history. Hence, it is always recommended that you maintain a healthy credit rating as an entrepreneur, as taking on debt can be less than ideal in times of need or when combatting unforeseeable circumstances.

Partnering With a Fintech Company

This is probably unorthodox, but there are benefits of partnering with a Fintech company if you are looking to acquire funds. A Fintech company is basically a financial institution that leverages technology and provides financial services to their target market. Hence, partnering with them can give you access to their expertise, such as utilizing their platforms, programs, and getting the initial funds to run your business.

You can approach Fintech companies for applying for a loan, and you can expect the business relationship to be conducted digitally. If you can win over a Fintech company with your brilliant idea and well-presented business plan, you are definitely on your way to opening up a new world of unimaginable opportunities for the future of your business.

Angel Investors

Angel investors are basically high-net-worth individuals who have the financial capacity to meet the financial needs of aspiring entrepreneurs, such as yourself, to fund their new business ventures. In return, they get a share of ownership in the business in the form of equity. This can totally depend on the type of business you are going to start, as angel investors look to analyze the type of investment and the level of participation they will require.

To impress an angel investor, your business idea should show signs of progression and value creation. Your business plan should be well presented and expand on the essential details you have learned about in Chapter 2. You can find angel investors by attending business networking events, participating in online forums, and asking around in your own network.

Personal Connections

I ended the previous point by recommending that you ask around in your own network of people. This leads me to the point that your personal connections may be another source for you to get the necessary funds to start your business venture. This includes taking out loans or offering equity options to your friends and family.

Getting loans from your personal connections can be easier compared to getting loans from external parties, but you will hold more accountability to repay the amount. In addition, there are some risks involved in this type of transaction, such as being unable to repay the loan and causing rifts in the relationship you have with your friends and family.

Presenting Your Business Plan

After you have identified where you can get your funds from, you can start planning your business plan pitch. Your business plan is your central tool for winning over investors, no matter who they are. Even if you are presenting a business plan as a guest lecturer to students in universities, they must be inspired by and enjoy reading your business plan. They should be convinced to the point that they would feel interested in taking some sort of stake in your venture.

Therefore, it is imperative to know who your audience is and keep them in mind. Making a good first impression will help you to sell your business idea. Here are a few steps that you can follow to prepare yourself for presenting your business plan.

Step 1: Get your leads and referrals.

The first move you need to make is to find all the names, addresses, and contact details of the investors you want to target. The above section should assist you with getting a good idea of the type of investors you want to focus your move on. You can get this information by searching online, networking with as many people as possible, and asking people in your personal space for referrals. Getting referrals is another effective way to find an ideal type of investor you want to prepare your pitch for.

Step 2: Learn about your target.

The next step is to research thoroughly and do a background check on the investors you wish to target. You can find a lot of information about their net worth so you have a good idea of how much money they have available to invest and whether it meets your funding requirements. You can research all this information online by searching forums or their personal websites, reading through news articles, and browsing through other sources.

Step 3: Draft the pitch.

An introductory pitch is crucial to introduce yourself and your intent in sending your business plan over for them to read over and analyze. People will be busy with their lives, and it can be a challenge to grab their attention. So, a hook is essential, and you should always get straight to the point to hook the investor and entice them to stay with you as you continue your pitch.

You can start by drafting an introductory email for your target in which you state that you have a business plan you want them to go through and share their thoughts on. You need to ask them if they would be interested in taking the next step and reading your plan. If you can make your email offer compelling enough, they will take some of their time to go through your plan. Be sure to mention that you are looking for someone to invest, some money to borrow, or to establish a business relationship for the long term. You can always mention where you got their contact information from, especially if it is a referral from a personal contact of yours.

Make sure you write your email to focus on the reader first by acknowledging their work and expertise before going in-depth about your business plan. It is always good to keep readers feeling engaged and appreciated about the work and status they've built before you ask for something. You should close your email by mentioning that you do require a response from them within a specified deadline. This way, you can save both your time and theirs should they not wish to continue with your pitch. In the case that you don't hear from them, you can always send two or three follow-up emails to check in with them before moving on to another target.

Step 4: Schedule a meeting.

After you are able to get your investor's attention and interest, make sure you schedule a meeting to meet them in person. Like I mentioned in the earlier chapters, meeting in person can increase your chances of connecting with people and winning them over. If this is not possible, no worries. Using video-conferencing tools such as Zoom, Skype, Google Meet, etc., can work. It is all about getting that first meeting and having a face-to-face conversation about the business plan and your funding requirements.

Step 5: Address all the objections.

During your meeting—whether in person or virtually—you should make sure you address any objections or doubts they have regarding the business venture. You might hear objections such as whether your company can survive against other top competitors, how you can guarantee you'll hit the revenue you have projected in your financial plan, and how you will carry out your management process. You will need to be ready to answer each objection one by one and provide an honest answer to all of them. In any business or personal relationship, you need to be transparent from the start to gain and maintain that long-term trust from your potential investors who will be funding your business venture throughout.

Step 6: Close the deal.

This is where you will hit the gas and go for it. Tell them what you need regarding all your funding requirements and get them to fully commit to an answer regarding your project. After dealing with their objections, try to get them to a decision as soon as possible. If they are impressed by your presentation, they will show no hesitation and will be ready to fund your project. No matter what the outcome might be— positive or negative—make sure you either close the deal or learn from your mistakes and apply those lessons the next time.

Approaching Banks and Lenders

Suppose you want to approach banks and other financial institutions in your quest for funding requirements. Writing a business plan that banks can't resist might be your ultimate dream, but you will be pleasantly surprised to learn that it is actually easier than you think. All you need to learn are the basic, essential details that banks and other lenders tend to focus on when deciding whether to approve loans. Once you've nailed these details and made sure they're presented in your plan, you'll be well on your way.

The objective here is to think from the bank's perspective and imagine that you are the bank official reading the business plan. What would you look at to make sure that you are giving out a loan to a business venture that will be profitable and from which you can expect repayment of the loan with interest? You need to be thinking from the risk management perspective as well. After all, banks are used to being approached by businesses who want them to finance their projects, so this isn't something that's new for them, and they will have a process in place for making decisions.

You may be surprised that banks aren't generally too interested in the shinier aspects, like your future expansion plans and growth potential. They prefer to stick to the basics in the interest of their institutions.

Here are a few things that bankers will take notice of so you can make them a focus as you prepare and present your business plan:

Business Cash Flow

This one shouldn't be a surprise, as cash flow is one of the best ways to convince bankers that you are going to be a sustainable and profitable business. When you have a good cash flow, it reduces the risk of defaulting on the loan (failure to pay back the loan), and banks can expect the repayment of the loan within the fixed time period. Hence, bankers will be very interested in seeing your projected cash flow statements, balance sheets, tax returns, and income statements or financial statements that you've prepared for the previous financial years, if you are an existing business.

Defined Funding Request

This goes back to what we learned regarding the Funding Request page in Chapter 2. This section of your business plan comes into play when you approach a banker or other financial institution. They will look specifically at the amount you are looking for, how you will use those funds, and any other detailed assessment of your funding requirements that might concern them. Therefore, ensure that this section of your business plan is written clearly to communicate the estimates for your initial funding needs that will be necessary to start operations immediately.

Collateral and Co-Signers

Another thing that banks may pay attention to is collateral. Collateral is something the bank can seize and keep hold of that belongs to you. This can be any of your assets, such equipment, inventory, machinery, or even your home. Banks can hold these assets and can sell them to get back all the money you have borrowed from them in the case of a default. Hence, banks will look for collateral, as they have surely been in the situation where entrepreneurs fail to meet their profits goals and struggle to make payments. They use collateral as leverage over you, and this is worth mentioning, as it should definitely come up in your discussion with them.

Another thing that offers protection for bankers is co-signers. A co-signer is someone who will bear the responsibility for paying back the loan should the primary borrower (in this case, the business owner like yourself) fail to pay it back. In most cases, a co-signer will be a family member or close friend of the borrower.

Management Plan

Bankers like to analyze and evaluate the management plans for a business. This is crucial, especially if you are a startup seeking funds. They will analyze whether your management plan is convincing and also run a background check on you as an individual. They will study your business history, credit rating, and your attributes regarding running a successful business. This can feel judgmental, but bankers must feel confident when they approve a loan to you. Your presentation skills and personality can shine here and convince them to offer that loan approval. Bankers simply won't approve loans if they see signs of bad management planning, as this can be a sign that you will struggle with leading your business to success and ultimately fail to repay the loan.

Marketing Plan

Without a doubt, your marketing plan is another aspect that will attract the eyes of the bankers. They will want to know about your key marketing activities that you have planned to reach out to customers and close sales. This is related to showing a healthy cash flow in your organization so bankers can analyze and discern whether your marketing activities will bode well when it comes to competing against other rivals in the market and acquiring clients quickly.

I Got One "Yes" ... Now What?

So, you got one yes. What should you do next? It is an amazing feeling to get a yes after reaching out to many investors or lenders and to settle an agreement to fulfill your funding requirements. First and foremost, this is a long process in itself, reaching out to many investors and going through hours of discussions to convince them. Second, it is crucial to get their verbal agreement on paper. So, your next step is to keep a written agreement ready in the event of someone agreeing to fund your business.

What details should I include in my written agreement?

Firstly, you should outline the terms. You start off by stating the official starting date for your project. You will specifically mention the day, the month, and the year that you will commence all your business operations. You can also include the termination date of the business here, depending on the type of business venture you are pursuing.

Second, you can outline all the roles and responsibilities of the parties involved in the agreement. This means defining your and other business partners' roles in the business and who will be held liable. You can outline the protocols for what to do in times of conflict or should disputes arise.

If you are offering equity in your proposal, you will outline the ownership details in this agreement—specifically, defining the percentage of share each party will get and their involvement level in the business. You can also illustrate the earning scheme for each owner, including how they will get paid and the percentage of profit after taxes that will be given to them.

Next, your written agreement should mention how members can join the business at any point and define their roles and participation in the venture. If there is no plan for accepting new admittance, then you should specify this clearly in the written agreement.

As for the details concerning withdrawal and dissolution, you will need to draft a clause in the agreement that defines the terms for any event of withdrawal and explain its process. In the event of the death of one of the owners, a business could be dissolved, but this should be stated clearly in the business agreement. All other details, such as assets allocated to owners and other parties, should be outlined here as well in the agreement.

It is best to get this written agreement ready in advance before you approach investors so you don't waste time after getting the yes. Make sure you have a lawyer ready and involved as well to ease this process for you. Eventually, you will be able to put forward their verbal agreement and finalize it on paper with their signature. At this point, you are all set and have successfully fulfilled your funding request.

Key Takeaways From This Chapter

- Selling your business plan is crucial in drafting a good pitch and reaching out to your ideal investors who can fulfill your funding request.
- Identify where your funds will be coming from. You can approach banks for business loans, get a business line of credit, approach angel investors, partner with Fintech companies, ask your friends and family and offer them an equity option, or ask for referrals.
- You should follow a step-by-step process for presenting your business plan. You will be required to determine your ideal investor, do research on your target, draft an introductory email pitch, book a meeting, address objections, and finalize the deal if

they are willing to commit to your project and provide funds.

- Bankers and other lenders will take notice of your cash flow, management plan, marketing plan, defined funding request section, collateral, and co-signers when you approach them with a funding request.
- When you get someone to agree to fund your project, you must get their verbal agreement down on paper by making them sign a written agreement which outlines all the terms and conditions.

Chapter 6

Business Plans for Common Businesses

Believe you can and you're halfway there.

— Theodore Roosevelt

The last few chapters have covered the key elements that make up a business plan, how to write each section well, and instilling the importance of pitching your business plan. It is now time to explore some business plan examples for different types of businesses.

The main purpose here is to offer some inspiration as you go through and analyze each example and how you might be able to use a similar style or strategy in your own writing. Another purpose for including examples is that I want you to understand and be able to recognize the minor differences between each business example relating to the type of business being put forward.

Even if you find the type of business you are planning to run in this list and go through its business plan example, I suggest you continue to read through the other examples as well to learn more about the other business models. This can help you pick up on what to include or exclude and customize your own business plan.

Disclaimer: All of the examples below contain figures and statistics that may not be accurate in the real world. The figures are included only for demonstration purposes regarding how to structure each section of your business plan. Do not take the financial figures or statistical data mentioned in the examples seriously or use the same numbers in your business plan. Do your own research, and you will find the appropriate facts and figures related to your market and industry. Moreover, all these examples are written in brief, and they are simply learning tools to illustrate the elements outlined in this book. In your own business plan, you will be including more information based on your research and the objectives of your business.

Business Plan Example for Local Businesses

InQ Coworking Solutions LLC

Executive Summary

Problem

Edmonton, Canada has a lot of startup businesses. As of 2021, over 1,000 companies have started their business in the past year. However, there is a lack of office space due to many being occupied by other companies and the rise of office rent in the crowded areas. This has rendered many businesses and entrepreneurs unable to start their venture due to the lack of office space to work with their teams. As a result, many of them end up having to host meetings and presentations in the discomfort of their own homes.

Value Proposition

I'd like to introduce our solution to the problem: coworking spaces. InQ Coworking Solutions aims to provide new small businesses and aspiring entrepreneurs with the opportunity to enhance their work productivity and achieve their business goals through the use of our coworking spaces and a work-friendly environment.

Market Analysis

In Edmonton, Canada, there has been a 15% increase of companies getting started every month. This has presented an opportunity to open coworking spaces in ideal locations to improve the convenience for work-related matters and also provide a good ambience for work productivity.

Competitive Analysis

We have identified two types of competitors that may challenge us and target the same customers.

- **Direct competitors**

Other coworking spaces that provide the same services as us. They are Wired Solutions, Edmonton's Incuspace, and Jeremy's Work Hours.

- **Indirect competitors**

Properties and institutions that allow businesses to open offices and maintain long-term stay there. They also affect our target customer base.

Richard Hedberg

Expected Projections

InQ Coworking Solutions strives to form strategic partnerships with landlords and offer coworking space to our target market. We aim to generate an annual revenue of over $250,000 from all our five coworking spaces spread across Edmonton in the first year. It is a huge task but feasible, according to our research and with proper utilization of resources.

Financing Requirements

When it comes to financing, we require a startup investment of around $700,000 and future expansion plans of establishing five coworking spaces in Edmonton. Brad Lee is the founder and will invest around $400,000 in the business. For the remaining initial funds ($300,000) and funds for future plans for the next five years, we will seek funding from banks or angel investors.

Company Description

Ownership Structure

InQ Coworking Solutions will commence its operations in July, 2023. Our business's legal structure is a Limited Liability Company (LLC). This is how the ownership structure is laid out in the organization:

- **Board of Directors**: Consists of directors that are major shareholders of the company.
- **CEO**: The main head to direct and manage strategic decisions for the business.
- **Head of Finance**: Oversees financial activities of the business.

- **Head of Operations**: Oversees day-to-day operations and manages different projects and coworking spaces in Edmonton.
- **Head of Marketing and Sales**: Responsible for marketing and sales initiatives and leading the sales and marketing teams for all coworking spaces.

Management Team

Brad Lee is an aspiring entrepreneur who has worked in the software industry in the past. He is the founder of InQ Coworking Solutions and will be the CEO. Liam Cooper will be the head of operations, as he has experience working as an operations manager for many retail chains. Veronica Andrews will be the head of marketing and sales. She has vast experience working as a marketing manager for Ed-tech companies. Lastly, John Gavinsky will be the head of finance. He is passionate about finance and has experience working as a finance manager for shipping companies.

Market Analysis

Problem to Solve

Edmonton, Canada has a lot of startup businesses. As of 2021, over 1,000 companies have started their business in the past year. However, there is a lack of office space due to many being occupied by other companies and the rise of office rent in the crowded areas. This has rendered many businesses and entrepreneurs unable to start their venture due to the lack of office space to work with their teams. As a result, many of them end up having to host meetings, and presentations in the discomfort of their own homes.

Target Market Size and Segments

In Edmonton, Canada, there has been a 15% increase in companies being started every month. This has presented an opportunity to open coworking spaces in ideal locations that will improve convenience for work-related matters and also provide a good ambience for work productivity.

We will be targeting demographics of both men and women between the ages of 18 and 60 who want to start their small businesses. We will also target freelancers who want to work in coworking spaces.

Competition

We have identified two types of competitors that may challenge us and target the same customers.

- **Direct competitors**

Other coworking spaces that provide the same services as us. They are Wired Solutions, Edmonton's Incuspace, and Jeremy's Work Hours.

- **Indirect competitors**

Properties and institutions that allow businesses to open offices and maintain long-term stays there. They also affect our target customer base.

Competitive Advantage

We have a competitive advantage over our competing rivals by having more coworking spaces in Edmonton for better reach and convenience. We will also provide better marketing efforts compared to our rivals, which we found during our research, as they barely reach out to their target market.

Products and Services

<u>Services</u>

This is a service-based business, and we provide:

- coworking space for individuals, freelancers, small businesses
- meeting rooms for companies to have a good place to conduct meetings and conferences

Marketing and Sales Plan

<u>First Stage</u>

We will conduct our marketing efforts by reaching out to landlords and properties for sale. Our objective is to own five properties or spaces to open up five coworking spaces in Edmonton. We will approach each landlord or owner by cold calling or exploring properties for sale online.

Estimated marketing budget = $20,000

<u>Second Stage</u>

After opening up coworking spaces, we will reach out to prospects by running ad campaigns online through social media sites like LinkedIn, Facebook, Instagram, Pinterest, etc. We will also open a YouTube channel to promote content and our business. We will also run traditional marketing methods by putting ads on posters and billboards across Edmonton.

Estimated marketing budget = $60,000

Financial Plan

Forecasted Financials

InQ Coworking Solutions strives to form strategic partnerships with landlords and offer coworking space to our target market. We aim to generate an annual revenue of over $250,000 from all our five coworking spaces spread across Edmonton in the first year. It is a huge task but feasible, according to our research and proper utilization of resources.

Revenue by year for the first five years is projected given in the chart below: (insert graphs portraying the financials)

Net profit (or loss) by year for the first five years is projected given in the chart below: (insert graphs portraying the financials)

*The revenue and profit is calculated from all five coworking spaces.

Financial Statements

Profit and loss statement for the first five financial years: (insert financial statement depicting figures)

Balance Sheet for the first five financial years: (insert financial statement depicting figures)

Cash flow statement for the first five financial years: (insert financial statement depicting figures)

*All these statements cover all five coworking spaces.

Financing

When it comes to financing, we require a startup investment of around $700,000 and future expansion plans of establishing five coworking spaces in Edmonton.

Usage of Funds

When it comes to investing our funds, we have estimated startup expenses for all five coworking spaces. We will incur costs in the following:

- registration and legal fees: $1,000
- insurance fees: $2,000
- rent to landlord: $50,000
- furniture: $45,000
- equipment: $35,000
- other costs: $15,000

Total Expenses = $148,000

Source of Funds

Brad Lee is the founder and will invest around $400,000 in the business. For remaining initial funds ($300,000) and funds for future plans for the next five years, we will seek funding from banks or angel investors.

Business Plan Example for an Ecommerce Business

E-Returns.com: Executive Summary

Problem

With the rise of ecommerce websites and transactions, many online merchants and suppliers need to process returns. There is a great deal of financial processing involved in every online transaction—whether it's the shipping of goods or receiving them. This year, the average rate of returns for all ecommerce-based companies hit about 10%. As a result, the value of returns was estimated to be around a whopping $2.3 billion.

Value Proposition

Introducing the solution—E-Returns.com. We strive to deliver a strategic solution for online merchants, shipping companies, and other web-hosting companies by handling free shipping of returned goods to customers. We will leverage our infrastructure, which utilizes software and AI, to provide a service that is quick and instantly solves issues among two or more online parties.

Market Analysis

Ecommerce continues to thrive, and there is an insane amount of money being spent on transactions each day. The growth seems stable, and there are no signs of it slowing down. Online revenue was estimated to be around $15 billion during the holiday season. The major market sectors included online shopping for electronics, apparel, books, home and garden supplies, and much more. With that many online merchants involved in different types of goods transactions, this signals a great opportunity.

Competitive Analysis

E-Returns.com identifies three variations of competition we could face for providing our services.

- **Direct Competitors**

These are our top competing delivery services like FEDEX.

- **Internal Competitors**

As E-Returns.com strives to provide every consumer with almost-free shipping, we have identified that the online retailers themselves will be our internal competition.

- **Channel Competitors**

When looking from a distribution channel perspective, there are service providers like PostNet that form business partnerships with several of these online retailers, so they are another variation of competition we need to keep our eye on.

Expected Projections

E-Returns.com aims to generate outstanding sales through this market opportunity and our financials look promising through the first three years at least. It all depends on whether we can form strategic partnerships with online merchants, and this will compound for better growth later on.

Financing Requirements

To finance the business, we require a total of $60,000 to begin operations. The three owners involved will put forward $20,000 each.

Company Description

Ownership Structure

E-Returns.com will divide its ownership structure based on the following responsibilities:

- Board of Directors: to oversee overall progress of the business and strategic decisions
- CEO: the main head to manage and make strategic decisions by utilizing resources, managing day-to-day business operations, and ensuring financial stability
- Director of Finance: to oversee responsibilities in safeguarding financial assets and human resources
- Director of Sales and Marketing: to oversee responsibilities to carry out marketing initiatives and generate sales
- Director of Information Technology: to protect and manage technology, software, and information resources

Management Team

There are three people responsible for starting this idea. E-Returns.com was founded by John Carrew, Ivan Pavlov, and Nathan King. John spent his years working for UPS in the delivery services. Ivan is an efficient IT consultant after his years in IBM, and Nathan has worked as an investment banker for Goldman Sachs. Using these three diverse minds and skill sets, E-Returns.com aims to deliver efficient customer service utilizing our virtual infrastructure.

Products and Services

Services

- Processing returns with online merchants and ecommerce transactions

- Providing customers with almost-free returns per transaction

Market Analysis

Problem to Solve

This year, the average rate of returns for all ecommerce-based companies hit about 10%. As a result, the value of returns was estimated to be around a whopping $2.3 billion. As ecommerce continues to thrive, there are also problems arising for merchants and other online delivery services regarding the processing of returns.

Target Market Size

The growth seems stable, and there are no signs of it slowing down. Online revenue was estimated to be around $15 billion during the holiday season. The major market sectors included online shopping for electronics, apparel, books, home and garden supplies, and much more. With that many online merchants involved in different types of goods transactions, this signals a great opportunity.

Market Segments

Our sources have indicated that merchants are successfully selling physical products such as electronics, apparel, books, etc. There was no inclusion of online services such as subscription-based models or online hotel-booking platforms.

Competition

E-Returns.com identifies three variations of competition we could face for providing our services:

- **Direct Competitors**

These are our top competing delivery services like FEDEX.

- **Internal Competitors**

As E-Returns.com strives to provide every consumer with almost-free shipping, we have identified that the online retailers themselves will be our internal competition.

- **Channel Competitors**

When looking from a distribution channel perspective, there are service providers like PostNet that form business partnerships with several of these online retailers, so they are another variation of competition we need to keep our eye on.

E-Returns.com can create a competitive advantage by leveraging merchants, consumers, and online communities to increase awareness, form strategic partnerships, and provide consumer service with ease.

Marketing and Sales Plan

Marketing Plan

The initial marketing initiative for us is to promote the business directly to online merchants. We can do this through direct selling and scheduling meetings to achieve our end goal—to form a strategic partnership. We can utilize email marketing campaigns to reach out as well. It is estimated that our costs for marketing for the first year will be around $650,000.

Sales Plan

E-Returns.com is aiming to form strategic partnerships with online merchants and other delivery and shipping companies through direct selling. It is estimated that we would need about $350,000 to run sales development programs and train our sales force. Our plan is to achieve a closing rate of at least 10% per month for the first year.

Key Metrics

- qualified leads
- active clients
- number of referrals
- number of customers who use our services per month
- number of returns handled
- website user interface interaction

Financial Plan

Forecasted Financials

Our aim is to maintain a $6 million investment and remain competitive in the years to come.

Our revenue by year is projected in the chart below: (insert graphs portraying the financials)

Our net profit (or loss) by year is projected in the chart below: (insert graphs portraying the financials)

Financial Statements

Here is our projected profit and loss statement for the first three financial years: (insert financial statement depicting figures)

Our projected balance sheet: (insert financial statement depicting figures)

Projected cash flow statement: (insert financial statement depicting figures)

Financing

When it comes to usage of funds, we have estimated startup expenses as the following:

- registration and legal: $250
- insurance: $200
- office rent: $750
- office stationery: $150
- equipment: $2,000
- marketing materials (business cards, brochures, etc.): $850
- other costs: $400

Total Expenses = $4,600

Source of Funds

To finance the business, we require a total of $60,000 to begin operations. The three owners involved will put forward $20,000 each.

Business Plan Example for an Innovative Business Idea

Gordon's Rental Homes: Executive Summary

Problem

The city of San Diego has seen a decline in attracting tourists. We have identified that there is a lack of short-term rental homes in the city where travelers can stay and spend time sightseeing. Short-term rental homes dominate almost 80% of the United States, but San Diego has a lack of rental homes. There is a demand and interest from tourists who want to spend time in San Diego, but they find it difficult to book short-term rental homes due to lack of options.

Value Proposition

Gordon's Rental Homes strives to provide tourists with short-term rental homes by utilizing the Airbnb platform. We aim to be a great Airbnb host and leverage the platform by delivering value to clients and giving them plenty of short-term rental home options to stay in.

Market Analysis

In the United States, Airbnb hosts dominate the market, with at least 23% of people per state being hosts and owning short-term rental homes. As of 2021, the Airbnb market has continued to grow, and property hosts globally have earned more than $180 billion solely from their renting activity, which is staggering. This is an opportunity for us to capitalize on the potential rental activity in San Diego.

Competitive Analysis

Gordon's Rental Homes has identified two types of competitors during our market research and analysis.

- **Direct competitors**

These will be our direct competing Airbnb hosts who are offering the same service as us and using the same platform.

- **Indirect competitors**

These are other short-term rental homeowners and hosts who offer similar services but are using other traditional marketing methods, such as listing on Craigslist or utilizing other hosting platforms.

Expected Projections

Gordon's Rental Homes aims to generate revenue through short-term renting by developing short-term rental homes and forming strategic partnerships with residents who are interested in renting out their homes. The projection looks promising due to the demand in San Diego and the growth of the Airbnb platform. In the first three years, we are seeking to cross over $1,500,000 in revenue and make about $756,984 of net profit.

Financing Requirements

To finance our business operations, we would need around $800,000 in startup investment and for future expansion plans for developing homes. Miles Gordon, owner of Gordon's Rental Homes, will invest around $250,000 in the business. We are looking to seek the remaining funds through bank loans or investors who are interested in joining our venture.

Company Description

Ownership Structure

Gordon's Rental Homes was founded in 2023, and it will begin operations this May. We have divided our ownership structure based on the following responsibilities:

- **CEO**: the main head to manage and make strategic decisions and lead operations as Airbnb host
- **Director of Finance:** in charge of overseeing responsibilities in protecting financial resources and tracking financial activity
- **Director of Sales and Marketing**: in charge of overseeing responsibilities to carry out marketing initiatives and generate sales
- **IT Head:** in charge of taking care of technical responsibilities regarding the business and frequently updating the digital activity of the business

Management Team

Miles Gordon is responsible for starting this business as the founder of Gordon's Rental Homes. He has experience working in real estate as an agent selling properties. His wife, Jenna Gordon, will be assisting as Director of Sales and Marketing. She has experience as a marketing manager in FMCG companies. Miles's brother, Davy Gordon, will be in charge of financial activities. He has a background of working as a chartered accountant and as a tax consultant. Alberto Jimenez, a good friend of Miles's, will be the IT head and will assist with digital and information technology-related activities.

Market Analysis

Problem to Solve

The city of San Diego has seen a decline in attracting tourists. We have identified that there is a lack of short-term rental homes in the city where travelers can stay and spend time sightseeing. Short-term rental homes dominate almost 80% of the United States, but San Diego has a lack of rental homes. There is a demand and interest from tourists who want to spend time in San Diego, but they find it difficult to book short-term rental homes due to lack of options.

Target Market Size and Segments

The Airbnb market continues to grow, and more customers are wanting to stay at short-term rentals and vacation homes with their friends and families. It looks promising indeed. There is huge demand in San Diego, and customers aged between 18 and 45 dominate the market segment.

Competition

Gordon's Rental Homes has identified two types of competitors during our market research and analysis.

- **Direct competitors**

These will be our direct competing Airbnb hosts who are offering the same service as us and using the same platform.

- **Indirect competitors**

These are other short-term rental homeowners and hosts who offer similar services but are using other traditional marketing methods, such as listing on Craigslist or utilizing other hosting platforms.

We can create a competitive advantage by leveraging home-owners and reaching out to them. This can save us money, and we can leverage our database to reach out to these residents more quickly than other Airbnb hosts.

Products and Services

Services

These are the following services we provide:

- high quality, short-term rental homes
- short-term rentals and vacation homes in San Diego
- consultation with homeowners and offers regarding equity to use their home for renting activities

Marketing and Sales Plan

Marketing Plan

The marketing effort is for us to reach out to as many home-owners as possible in San Diego. We can utilize our database to get contact information and use cold calling to reach them directly. We also plan to run ad campaigns online through social media, especially in Facebook groups, to reach out to them. We are also looking to form strategic partnerships with other developers, so we will run ad campaigns on LinkedIn. Later, we will reach out to customers utilizing the power of the Airbnb platform by optimizing our profile and posting quality photographs of homes on the site. We will seek out paid advertising if at all possible. The total estimated budget for carrying out our marketing activities would be around $38,000 for the first year.

<u>Sales Plan</u>

Our sales strategy involves direct selling and convincing homeowners to rent out their homes on Airbnb. We will follow the sales model of prospecting, screening qualified leads, booking a discovery call, setting up face-to-face meetings, and closing the deal after two or three rounds of negotiating. We will have a sales team that consists of 10 or more individuals who will be provided with training and who will reach out to homeowners during our initial stages of the business. We will later reach out to potential tourist prospects and refer them to our Airbnb profile to book homes with us.

Financial Plan

<u>Forecasted Financials</u>

Our revenue by year for the first three years is projected in the chart below: (insert graphs portraying the financials)

Our net profit (or loss) by year for the first three years is projected in the chart below: (insert graphs portraying the financials)

<u>Financial Statements</u>

Here is our projected profit and loss statement for the first three financial years: (Insert financial statement depicting figures)

Our projected balance sheet: (insert financial statement depicting figures)

Projected cash flow statement: (insert financial statement depicting figures)

<u>Financing</u>

Usage of Funds

When it comes to investing our funds, we have estimated startup expenses as the following:

- registration and legal: $300
- insurance: $175
- office rent: $500
- office stationery and equipment: $1,000
- marketing materials (business cards, brochures, etc.): $200
- IT-related costs: $500
- other costs: $350

Total Expenses = $3,025

For expenses related to preparing and maintaining one Airbnb home for the first year, here is the breakdown of expenses:

- rent to homeowner: $45,000
- home insurance: $12,000
- cleaning supplies and amenities: $35,000
- salaries paid to cleaning crew: $20,000
- salaries paid to repair and maintenance crew: $10,000
- furniture and other amenities: $45,000
- security systems and installation: $15,000
- marketing: $8,000

Total Expenses = $190,000

Source of Funds

To finance our business operations, we would need around $800,000 for startup investment and future expansion plans for developing homes. Miles Gordon, owner of Gordon's Rental Homes, will invest around $250,000 in the business. We are looking to seek the remaining funds through bank loans or investors who are interested in joining our venture.

Business Plan Example for Influencer Business

Katy's Skincare Sundays: Executive Summary

Problem

The skincare industry is big, but there has been less educational content and more promotion recently, especially in the YouTube and Instagram spaces. The goal is to provide educational content for the target market who want to maintain a proper skincare routine.

Value Proposition

Katy's Skincare Sundays is an initiative focusing on providing content to the target market regarding a skincare routine, products, and personal experiences to lift their confidence. The aim is to deliver value by providing continuous content (every Sunday on YouTube) and building a wide audience online.

Market Analysis

In the United States alone, over 1.3 million women spend money on products for their skincare routine. Globally, as of 2022, there has been an estimated $2.3 billion in skincare product sales. This spells opportunity for marketers but with a lot of competition; the aim is to deliver educational content and value first before promoting products.

Competitive Analysis

Two types of competitors (influencers) were identified:

- **Direct competitors**

Influencers online who are already providing educational content and marketing skincare routine products.

- **Indirect competitors**

Influencers who are in the beauty niche but provide more than just skincare products. They also provide cosmetics, hair care products, apparel, etc.

Expected Projections

We are expecting to generate around $35,000 in YouTube ad revenue in the first year if we maintain a strict marketing content strategy for the calendar year. It is also estimated that we will generate around $20,000 in affiliate sales and direct selling for the first year if we partner with enough skincare product companies and get sponsorship deals from some of them.

Financing Requirements

To cover startup costs, there is a requirement of at least $5,000 to start providing content straightaway.

Company Description

Company Overview

This is an influencer business founded and run by Kathy Olsen. She is a health and fitness enthusiast, and she has a passion for her skincare routine. She was born and raised in Sweden before moving to the United States in 2016.

Management Team

Kathy Olsen will be the CEO of the influencer business and will be the face of the YouTube channel and Instagram profiles. She will be assisted by two more individuals who will form the management team. Shirley Davis will be in charge of content management and marketing. She went to art school and has experience working as a freelance video script writer. Jenna Newton will be in charge of public relations and a liaison between different brands and companies offering sponsorships. She has experience working as a PR officer for two reputable companies.

Market Analysis

Problem to Solve

The skincare industry is big, but there has been less educational content and more promotion recently, especially in the YouTube and Instagram spaces. The goal is to provide educational content for the target market who want to maintain a proper skincare routine.

Target Market Size and Segments

In the United States alone, over 1.3 million women spend money on products for their skincare routine. Globally, as of 2022, there has been an estimated $2.3 billion in skincare product sales. This spells opportunity for marketers but with a lot of competition; the aim is to deliver educational content and value first before promoting products.

The target market strategy involves positioning our content to cater to women aged between 18 and 40, specifically.

<u>Competition</u>

Two types of competitors (influencers) were identified:

- **Direct competitors**

Influencers online who are already providing educational content and marketing skincare routine products.

- **Indirect competitors**

Influencers who are in the beauty niche but provide more than just skincare products. They also provide cosmetics, hair care products, apparel, etc.

Competitive Advantage

Katy's Skincare Sundays can create an advantage with a brand position of being a skincare routine show every Sunday. We aim to provide lots of content consistently, especially regarding shows every Sunday so that our target audience builds a habit of tuning in and looking forward to our educational content on that particular day.

Products and Services

<u>Products</u>

After building a large audience, our plan is to promote products on the channel and other platforms after the sixth month of the first year. These skincare products will include:

- moisturizers
- creams
- face masks
- toners
- face washes and scrubs
- facial wipes
- body wash
- perfumes

We also plan to promote and sell:

- skincare-related books
- personal books
- webinars

Services

Our focus is primarily aimed at:

- providing high-quality and consistent educational content regarding skincare routines.
- providing 1-on-1 consultation sessions for health and fitness, as well as skincare routines.

Marketing and Sales Plan

Marketing Plan

Our marketing plan is to create content in the form of videos on YouTube, prepare infographics, and share personal photos and clips on social media. We will also create short viral clips and market them on TikTok for better reach. The total estimated budget for running these activities will be around $2,000.

Sales Plan

We will reach out to skincare companies and brands to form strategic alliances, and we will rely on our sales mainly through affiliate sales by promoting their products through our channel and other platforms. We estimate about $750 for sales-related activities.

Key Metrics

- number of subscribers
- number of views
- number of clicks on affiliate links
- number of subscriptions
- number of sponsorship deals

Financial Plan

Forecasted Financials

Revenue by year for the first three years is projected in the chart below: (insert graphs portraying the financials)

This is a multi-graph chart with a breakdown of revenue from YouTube ad revenue, affiliate sales, sponsorship deals, and other sources: (insert chart)

Net profit (or loss) by year for the first three years is projected in the chart below: (insert graphs portraying the financials)

This is a multi-graph chart with a breakdown of net profit from YouTube ad revenue, affiliate sales, sponsorship deals, and other sources: (insert charts)

Financial Statements

This is the projected profit and loss statement for the first three financial years: (insert financial statement depicting figures)

This is the projected balance sheet: (insert financial statement depicting figures)

This is the projected cash flow statement: (insert financial statement depicting figures)

Financing

Usage of Funds

We will invest startup funds for the following:

- camera: $1,500
- equipment: $1,250
- laptops: $1,750
- video editing software: $100
- marketing materials: $200
- other costs: $300

Total Expenses = $5,000

Source of Funds

To cover startup costs, there is a requirement of at least $5,000 to start providing content straightaway. To maintain operations with our content marketing and payment of salaries to employees, we will require an additional $20,000 for the first year, which will be covered by Kathy Olsen.

Business Plan Example for a Non-Profit Organization

Home Care Shelters: Executive Summary

<u>Problem</u>

In the U.S., there has been a huge rise in low-income, single-parent families who are not getting adequate housing. Over the past five years, over 23% of single-parent families with low-income jobs have lost their homes.

<u>Value Proposition</u>

Home Care Shelters is a nonprofit organization that strives to deliver housing to low-income, single-parent families. We have vast experience in the hospitality and social service industries prior to the formation, and have great connections with nearby communities. Our CEO also has experience working in the real estate business and has several business connections that help to organize development of housing facilities.

<u>Market Overview</u>

According to a recent United States 2022 report, almost 50% of homeless people have families with children and suffer from starvation. The poverty level rises every year, and this has been tracked with statistics going back almost 60 years ago. To relieve some portion of this poverty cycle, Home Care Shelters is ready to assist and shelter single parents with housing facilities. This is a long-term commitment that we feel passionate about.

<u>Future Plan</u>

Home Care Shelters is aiming to purchase real estate in areas where there are a majority of low-income, single-parent families looking to rent housing at a rate of 25% of the family's household income.

Financing Requirements

Home Care Shelters is looking to finance operations through accepting donations and contributions from the local government and other organizations.

Company Description

Company Overview

Home Care Shelters will be based in the state of New York and will provide homeless, single-parent families with their housing needs. This organization was founded by Rhett Wilson, who has vast experience in real estate development.

Management Team

There are three people who will act as the main heads in the organization. Rhett Wilson is the founder and will be CEO of the nonprofit organization. Nancy Davis will be the COO (Chief Operating Officer), and Brad Johnson will be the CFO (Chief Financial Officer). The management team has a background in the social service industry, with the founder and CEO having vast experience in real estate development, which will aid in serving our value proposition of building homes.

Products and Services

Products

- properties and housing for low-income, single-parent families
- real estate resources and expertise for contracting companies

Market Analysis

Problem to Solve

In the U.S., there has been a huge rise in low-income, single-parent families who are not getting adequate housing. Over the past five years, over 23% of single-parent families with low-income jobs have lost their homes.

Target Market Size

According to a recent United States 2022 report, almost 50% of homeless people have families with children and suffer from starvation. The poverty level rises every year, and this has been tracked with statistics going back almost 60 years ago. To relieve some portion of this poverty cycle, Home Care Shelters is ready to assist and shelter single parents with housing facilities. This is a long-term commitment that we feel passionate about.

Marketing Plan

Home Care Shelters will aim to focus their marketing efforts on the usage of national networks and social service parties. Using referrals and in-house marketing team campaigns, we will look to promote our services both online and offline.

Key Metrics

- qualified leads

- active partners
- number of referrals
- number of homeless families served per month
- number of real estate projects running
- website user interface interaction

Financial Plan

Forecasted Financials

Home Care Shelters has prepared financials for the first three years.

Year 1: Estimated about $734,328 in startup costs for launching up to seven housing projects.

Year 2: Estimated about $5,324,435 for completing first capital raise.

Year 3: Estimated about $9,473,000 for completing $5 million raise in capital.

Financing

Source of Funds

Home Care Shelters is looking to finance operations through accepting donations and contributions from the local government and other organizations.

Business Plan Example for an Existing Business

VIVO Sports: Executive Summary

Problem

Physical education, and especially sports, is being overlooked in Canada, with many schools failing to entice children to take part in sports or organize inter-school tournaments. Twenty-five percent of children's parents in the state of British Columbia have stressed their disappointment in how their son or daughter is unable to receive sporting scholarships or sign up with youth academies of popular sports clubs. The number of youth players getting drafted into NFL teams and MLS teams from British Columbia keeps declining each year—by at least 40% in the last decade between 2011 to 2021. There is a need for infrastructure to organize sporting events that can help children participate and increase their chances of getting scholarships.

Value Proposition

VIVO Sports' primary function is to provide event management services for schools, universities, academies, and private institutions that are unable to organize sporting events themselves. Our aim is to ensure that kids gain access to sporting activities through their institutions so they can better themselves and have fun. We bridge the gap by providing institutions that have a lack of resources and time with the use of our resources and expertise to manage sporting events and competitions smoothly.

Market Analysis

With youth now shifting toward e-sports gaming, they are slowly losing connection with physical sports, and this has been a cause for alarm regarding the well-being and physical health of kids in our community.

Competitive Analysis

VIVO Sports has identified the emergence of two competing rivals who provide sporting event services. This has piqued our interest, since we were the first business to organize tournaments in British Columbia, and this has encouraged two new competitors to enter the market. The two competitors are SportsEx Ltd. and FootLock. They both offer event management and sporting tournament organization. FootLock mainly specializes in organizing football tournaments for schools and universities, but SportsEx Ltd. offers similar services as us.

Expected Projections

VIVO Sports has crossed over $500,000 in annual revenue in its first five years of formation. We are now aiming to generate better sales through our merchandising activities, and also maintain our primary business of organizing sporting events with focus and commitment. In the next five years, we will aim to cross over $1,500,000 in revenue with our latest strategic initiatives.

Financing Requirements

To finance our working capital to expand our business operations, we would require around $250,000. We are looking to seek funds from banks by asking for a business credit line.

Company Description

Company Overview

VIVO Sports was founded in 20xx and is based in British Columbia. It was founded by two friends—Jake Wilson and Owen Tyler—who are passionate soccer fans and have identified a market where they can organize sporting events to assist educational institutions. They want children and young adults to be able to play their favorite sports. The business's legal structure is based on a partnership between the two—where Jake owns 51% of the company and Owen owns 49%.

<u>Management Team</u>

Jake Wilson and Owen Tyler are the co-founders and are primarily responsible for making strategic business decisions. They recruited two more friends into the squad in their first year of formation based on their background and experience. Jordan Mackie is VIVO Sports' Chief Financial Officer due to his corporate experience from working in the banking sector. Ben Dorsey is the Chief Marketing Manager, as he has experience working in several marketing agencies in both the U.S. and Canada. These four form the heart of the business management team that has led VIVO Sports to great heights in the last five years.

Products and Services

<u>Products</u>

VIVO Sports has released the following products (merchandise):

- football jerseys
- soccer jerseys
- basketball jerseys
- baseball jerseys
- athletic gear
- running shoes

<u>Services</u>

VIVO Sports has been primarily a service-based business since its formation, and we offer the following:

- organization of inter-school sporting tournaments for schools, universities, and private institutions
- organization of training facilities for schools and universities
- consultation services for educational institutions
- strategic partnerships and services for sporting kit suppliers

Market Analysis

Problem to Solve

Twenty-five percent of children's parents in British Columbia have stressed their disappointment that their sons and daughters are unable to receive sporting scholarships or sign up with youth academies of popular sports clubs. The number of youth players getting drafted into NFL teams and MLS teams from British Columbia has been declining each year—by at least 40% in the last decade between 2011 to 2021. There is a need for new infrastructure and organization for sporting events to help children participate and increase their chances of getting scholarships.

Target Market Size and Segment

There are 30.3 million students in British Columbia, and this presents an opportunity for each one of them to get exposure to playing sports and receiving physical education. The main target segments include students between 13 and 18 years of age, for middle school and high school. We are also targeting young adults between the ages of 18 and 29 in universities and other private institutions.

<u>Competition</u>

VIVO Sports has identified the emergence of two competing rivals who provide sporting event services. This has piqued our interest, since we were the first business to organize tournaments in British Columbia, and this has encouraged two new competitors to enter the market. The two competitors are SportsEx Ltd. and FootLock. They both offer event management and sporting tournament organization. FootLock mainly specializes in organizing football tournaments for schools and universities, but SportsEx Ltd. offers similar services as us.

Marketing and Sales Plan

VIVO Sports' marketing plan was to promote the business directly by reaching out to educational institutions. We did this by cold calling, cold emailing, and making visits. We ran ad campaigns, and our marketing efforts have incurred costs of around $125,000 in the last five years.

Our sales team continues to aggressively close deals, and we aim to achieve at least a 20% closing rate per quarter every year.

<u>Key Metrics</u>

- qualified leads
- active projects
- number of referrals
- number of orders placed for merchandise
- website user interface interaction

Financial Plan

<u>Previous and Forecasted Financials</u>

Our revenue by year is given in the chart below. This is for the last five years: (insert graphs portraying the financials)

Our net profit (or loss) by year is given in the chart below. This is for the last five years: (insert graphs portraying the financials)

Our revenue by year is projected in the chart below. This is for the next five years since the introduction of merchandise selling and more strategic partnerships being formed: (insert graphs portraying the financials)

Our net profit (or loss) by year is projected in the chart below. This is for the next five years since the introduction of merchandise selling and more strategic partnerships being formed: (insert graphs portraying the financials)

<u>Financial Statements</u>

Here is our profit and loss statement for the first five financial years: (insert financial statement depicting figures)

Here is our profit and loss statement projected for the next five financial years: (insert financial statement depicting figures)

Here is our balance sheet for the first five financial years: (insert financial statement depicting figures)

Here is our balance sheet projected for the next five financial years: (insert financial statement depicting figures)

Here is our cash flow statement for the first five financial years: (insert financial statement depicting figures)

Here is our cash flow statement projected for the next five financial years: (insert financial statement depicting figures)

Financing

Usage of funds

We have planned for our funds to be invested in developing inventory control for our merchandising business, and we continue to use funds for our service-based activities.

Source of Funds

Initially, the co-owners invested a total of $800,000 into the company, with each sharing $400,000 among themselves. For our expansion plans, we need to finance our working capital to expand our business operations. This means we would require around $250,000 to maintain operations. We are looking to seek funds through asking banks for a business credit line.

Chapter 7

Business Planning Mistakes and How to Overcome Them

The price of inaction is far greater than the cost of a mistake.

— Meg Whitman

You have learned the basic elements that make up a business plan. You know how to write each section of your plan, and you've gone through examples of various business plans. You are now set to write your own business plan. However, most entrepreneurs go through their journey with a fair share of mistakes, and sometimes they get demotivated by the whole experience and hesitate when it comes time to make big decisions regarding their business.

This happened to me, too, and it is natural that you encounter the same anxiety from time to time. Nevertheless, it is important that you not give up on your dreams and keep pursuing them. You can overcome many mistakes by doing thorough research and writing your business plan properly, with all the sections written clearly and concisely. In a matter of time, you will get those funds secured because your hard work in conducting proper research and writing a great business plan draft will pay off.

This chapter will go through the common business planning mistakes that many make and how you can avoid them. Taking precautions will be helpful in the long run, as it will save you both time and energy. So let's dive straight in.

Common Business Plan Mistakes to Avoid

Over-Planning Can Be Dangerous

The first common mistake is using the term "planning" as an excuse to procrastinate and not take action when it's time. This can happen in two ways. One way is you have all these ideas of starting a business. You have planned the necessary steps and procedures that will make your business successful and profitable in the eyes of the investors. However, your multiple phases of planning lead to procrastination and you end up failing to finish the business plan. This can be one of the biggest mistakes you can make. You must remember that without a business plan, your path to success just becomes more difficult.

The other way someone can procrastinate is when, after planning everything in their business plan, they end up not taking any action and not completing any of the necessary steps, such as finding an investor, funding their business, and starting operations. Why does this happen? Because insecurity creeps in, and one can feel, after all that planning and drafting of the business plan, like this project may not work out for some reason. If that sounds like you, don't worry about it. It happens to many people at first.

Richard Hedberg

The best thing you can do is make your business plan a priority, and then focus your efforts on landing that loan or funding requirement. Your small actions will lead to positive changes, and trust me, it really does make a difference as you focus each day. When you leave yourself procrastinating and absorbing all that negative energy wrapped in your head, you will eventually become inactive and unable to make your business venture dreams come true.

Being Unrealistic with Projections

The next mistake you can make, and something I learned is very common, is when you are unrealistic about your projections and too optimistic. This can happen due to insufficient research or failing to accept the harsh facts about your competition and the income potential in your industry or target market. This comes back to the advice that you need to carry out proper research before estimating realistic projections for your business model. For instance, when it comes to your financial projections, do not look to overestimate and inflate your earning projections for the first few years.

I say this because if you put some unrealistic numbers in your projections, bankers won't take you seriously and they won't trust you enough to lend you money, as they will perceive you as someone who has not done the research and doesn't have the industry knowledge to estimate accurately. And for your own sake, if you are too optimistic and put forward unrealistic financial projections, you are most likely going to be subjected to high risks if a bank does lend you that money; you could end up defaulting and heading toward bankruptcy.

Overlooking Your Competitors

Another big mistake one can make is believing that you have minimal competition in your industry. Or, in the worst case, you believe there are no competitors to worry about. This can happen due to, yet again, lack of research, or being too optimistic about your business's success without taking into consideration the competition's capabilities. In short, you underestimate the hell out of your competitors. Always go into the business world with the mindset that you are in it to compete with others and go for the prize. Your target market are the ones with luxury at their feet—they have a lot of options to choose from for where they will spend their money. You have to accept that getting their attention will be a challenge, and you should respect your competing rival's business capabilities. You can use this lesson to your advantage by thoroughly analyzing your competitor's strengths and weaknesses and then leveraging all the good features in your own product or service framework.

Lack of Market Research

Without a doubt, as this has been mentioned a few times now, lack of market research can lead to many of these problems. It won't matter if you are willing to deliver value propositions and go through all the work to build that perfect product or service strategy. If there is no one willing to buy it, it is not worth selling. This can happen if you don't research your target market beforehand and understand their pain points. This was stressed many times in the earlier chapters, but it is best to bring it back up in this discussion again because planning is everything when it comes to leading a successful business.

Poorly Written Executive Summary

As discussed in Chapter 2, your Executive Summary is the introductory pitch that sets the tone and entices the reader to continue reading your business plan. For busy people like investors and lenders, who sacrifice their time to read your business plan, your Executive Summary tells them at first glance whether this venture is worth getting into. Many entrepreneurs make mistakes by drafting poor summaries that fail to impress, so potential investors don't even finish reading the whole plan.

Your business plan might be written well and contain all the information that will convince your investor or lender, but if your Executive Summary doesn't hook the reader, then you lose the entire business plan right there. It is like marketing. You may have a very good product or service you want to offer, but if your email subject line doesn't compel prospects to take action, then they will never open your email and never get to know more about your value proposition.

It may sound harsh, but that is the purpose of summaries in a business plan. Follow the tips that were discussed in Chapter 2 about writing concisely, and add the essential details for the summary. Put the time in and do everything right to present a good Executive Summary to entice your readers early on.

Making Your Business Plan Difficult to Comprehend

Sometimes, the problem can be in the writing itself. The presentation might be all wrong and the reader simply doesn't enjoy reading your business plan despite all the information you've given. For instance, your business plan might be too long, and it could test your readers' attention span. It might contain wordy content, redundant information, and irrelevant research data and resources.

To avoid such a situation, make it presentable by limiting your business plan to between five and ten pages long. Include graphs or charts to tell the story regarding financials. Additionally, make your sentences and paragraphs short and concise. Eliminate large blocks of text, and define each paragraph under headers and subheaders for readers to scan your business plan easily and comprehend the information better.

Furthermore, you might be subjected to making mistakes related to typos, grammar, and using wrong or inappropriate words. All of this should be avoided, and you must make your business plan look professional. Run your business plan through online tools such as Grammarly or Hemingway Editor to correct these mistakes. These are free and reliable online tools that can correct your spellings, fix grammatical errors, and also suggest improvements to write your sentences better.

Failing to Include Financials

Another mistake one can make is not including financial information in their business plan. Whenever you are making projections in your business plan, you must back up what you write. Hence, you need to include financials that are backed by market research and utilize data and references. Present your financial statements using charts and diagrams for better storytelling and presentation.

Always ensure you support all your claims with reliable data and the inclusion of financials. This is crucial not only to back up your claims but also for bankers and lenders to approve your loan, as they will look at this part carefully when reading your business plan.

Not Defining the Management Plan Accurately

Another major mistake one can make is not defining everyone's role and style of management in the company. It is crucial to define the management structure properly and address the conditions regarding recruiting talent by looking at educational backgrounds and experience. You will need to define who will be the board members and how each department will be managed, then you can address all the challenges and characteristics of your team as you look to achieve organizational goals.

Making Someone Else Write the Business Plan for You

Another mistake that one can make is delegating the task of writing the business plan to someone else. This is a huge red flag and must be avoided at any cost. You don't need to be the best professional writer out there to draft your business plan. Business plan writing comes from within, and your passion will drive its creation. You are the person who knows best the ins and outs of your business idea, your business model, the management style, the operations, marketing and sales plan, the financial plans, and other details that go into the business plan. When you outsource this task to someone —even if they are professional—you are not going to get that same feeling as you would if you had written it. It is simple and non-negotiable. You are the sole reason for starting the business, and you must write the business plan. And, as mentioned earlier when you started reading this book, you need to write down everything from scratch by yourself so that you end up committing to your words and taking actions to start your business. Embrace the psychology of writing a business plan, and use your heart and passion to construct a powerful and exciting text.

Being Overly Optimistic About Success

It is quite natural that some entrepreneurs fall into the trap of overexcitement. They learn about businesses and then start believing in the get-rich-quick scheme. Let me tell you, and you've probably heard this many times, but Rome wasn't built in a day. You have to put in the hours in this line of business and see the results for yourself after you've put in the effort and done things in a systematic way.

To avoid getting overwhelmed, nervous, burned out, or impatient with the hard stuff, always focus on enjoying the journey you are on as an entrepreneur. When you let yourself enjoy the adventure, things become easier for you. Hard and mundane work won't be seen as chores to you anymore, and you will end up looking forward to each day as you get closer to achieving your goals.

Key Takeaways From This Chapter

- Anyone can make mistakes when doing business planning, but it is all about learning from the mistakes and avoiding common mistakes to help you save time and energy and get closer to your goals.
- Never fall into the procrastination trap of planning so much that you end up forgetting or avoiding taking action.
- Do not overestimate things by setting unrealistic and inflated financial projections, ignoring competition, and taking things for granted.
- Lack of sufficient market research can lead to many of your business planning problems that arise and can even lead you to pursue the wrong business venture. Hence, always make sure you spend time on thorough market research.

- Writing your business plan properly is crucial. Make it readable and comprehensible. Moreover, your Executive Summary must be written well so that it attracts potential investors and lenders at first glance and they continue reading your whole plan.
- Look to include financials, and properly define your management style to convince readers about your project.
- Never outsource your business plan writing and use your passion and heart to write it yourself. It is your idea, after all.
- Never believe that success is easy. It takes a lot of work and time to see that empire grow. Always look to enjoy the entrepreneurial journey, and celebrate each milestone along the way.

Conclusion

The goal isn't more money. The goal is living life on your terms.

— Will Rogers

You have now reached the end of the journey of reading this book, but you're only just getting started in your entrepreneurial journey. Use the lessons you've learned in this book and your new understanding of the business plan to test yourself and move forward.

To summarize, this is what we have learned in this book:

- You've learned what a business model is and the different types of business models you can use to base your business on.
- You've learned about the important elements and key details to include in your business plan, including your Executive Summary, Company Description, Market Analysis, Marketing and Sales

Plan, Financial Plan and Projections, Funding Request Page, and Appendix.

- You've learned how you can utilize various strategies to grow your customer base and profit from a sustainable business.
- You've learned about the key resources, different types of key resources, and how you can determine your key resources based on your business model.
- You've learned how you can pitch your business plan and approach your ideal investor or lender to get a "yes" to your funding request.
- You've studied different business plan examples for different types of businesses.
- You've learned about the common mistakes you can make when creating a business plan, or when planning a business in general, and how you can overcome them.

This knowledge was important for me to share with you, as I want you to follow the same journey to success. Believe that your business can succeed if you organize your ideas and implement the right strategies.

A business plan is only the first step, but also one of the most important steps in building a successful business empire. And that's why this book focuses on business plans, so you can kickstart your entrepreneurial journey.

If you loved and enjoyed reading this content, do leave a review and share it with others who may need it as well. This information will help anyone to craft a business plan, even if they are baffled about where to start. Use these lessons to your advantage and apply them in your life, and you will see those positive changes coming through gradually.

Thank You

I want to give a big thank you to everyone who has bought my book. I hope you enjoyed the book and found it helpful.

If you could please take a moment to write a review on the platform, it would mean a lot to me. Your reviews help other people find my work and enjoy it, too. It will also help me write the kind of books that will help you get the results you want in your business.

Thanks again for taking the time to read my work and I hope to hear from you soon!

>> Leave a review on Amazon US <<
>> Leave a review on Amazon UK <<

References

3 Sample Nonprofit Business Plans for Inspiration [Updated 2022]. (2021, December 26). Growthink. https://www.growthink.com/businessplan/help-center/sample-nonprofit-business-plans

20 Reasons Why You Need a Business Plan in 2021. (2020, September 23). Growthink. https://www.growthink.com/content/20-reasons-why-you-need-business-plan#:~:text=The%203%20most%20important%20purposes

50 small business quotes to inspire you. (n.d.). IWOCA. https://www.iwoca.co.uk/insights/50-small-business-quotes/

AG, S. (2019). *Key Resources - Business Model Canvas | Strategyzer.* Strategyzer. https://www.strategyzer.com/business-model-canvas/key-resources

Business Plan 101: Sales & Marketing. (n.d.). Score. https://www.score.org/resource/blog-post/business-plan-101-sales-marketing#:~:text=The%20sales%20and%20marketing%20section

Caramela, S. (2018, September). *How to Connect With Customers.* Business News Daily. https://www.businessnewsdaily.com/10330-connect-with-customers.html

Choksi, N. (2021, September 30). *5 Ways A New Business Owner Can Get Working Capital.* Forbes Advisor INDIA. https://www.forbes.com/advisor/in/business-loans/5-ways-a-new-business-owner-can-get-working-capital/

E-Commerce Start-Up Business Plan - Financial Plan - Bplans: Business Planning Resources and Free Business Plan Samples. (n.d.). Bplans: Free Business Planning Resources and Templates. https://www.bplans.com/e-commerce-start-up-business-plan/financial-plan/

Fox, G. (2020, January 3). *Key Resources - 5 Essential Resources For A Successful Business Model - Www.garyfox.co.* GARY FOX. https://www.garyfox.co/business-model/key-resources/

Hargrave, M. (2019, April 23). *Customer Relationship Management - CRM Goes beyond Just Software.* Investopedia. https://www.investopedia.com/terms/c/customer_relation_management.asp

How to Maintain Customer Relationships and Build Loyalty. (n.d.). Square. https://squareup.com/us/en/townsquare/maintain-customer-relationships-and-build-loyalty

163

References

How to Write a Company Overview for a Business Plan. (n.d.). NerdWallet. https://www.nerdwallet.com/article/small-business/company-overview

How to Write an Ecommerce Business Plan [Examples & Template]. (n.d.). Blog.hubspot.com. https://blog.hubspot.com/marketing/ecommerce-business-plan

How to Write an Executive Summary in 6 Steps. (n.d.). NerdWallet. https://www.nerdwallet.com/article/small-business/executive-summary

How To Write an Executive Summary With Example. (n.d.). The Balance. https://www.thebalancemoney.com/business-plan-executive-summary-example-2948007

How to Write a Market Analysis for a Business Plan. (n.d.). NerdWallet. https://www.nerdwallet.com/article/small-business/market-analysis

How To Write the Products and Services Section of Your Business Plan. (n.d.). The Balance. https://www.thebalancemoney.com/business-plan-format-1794224

Inc, T. S. of E. M. (2014, November 13). *How to Write a Business Plan Banks Can't Resist.* Entrepreneur. https://www.entrepreneur.com/starting-a-business/how-to-write-a-business-plan-banks-cant-resist/238928

Inc, T. S. of E. M. (2015, February 3). *6 Strategies for Presenting Your Business Plan.* Entrepreneur. https://www.entrepreneur.com/starting-a-business/6-strategies-for-presenting-your-business-plan/241539

Kopp, C. M. (2020, July 3). *Understanding Business Models.* Investopedia. https://www.investopedia.com/terms/b/businessmodel.asp

Lesonsky, R. (2020). *10 Ways to Get New Customers.* SBA. https://www.sba.gov/blog/10-ways-get-new-customers

Nandwani, S. (n.d.). *Council Post: A Beginner's Guide To Planning Your Entrepreneurial Journey.* Forbes. https://www.forbes.com/sites/forbesbusinesscouncil/2022/10/24/a-beginners-guide-to-planning-your-entrepreneurial-journey/?sh=21982f4052be

Nicastro, S., & Murphy, R. (2022, July 26). *How to Write a Business Plan, Step by Step.* NerdWallet. https://www.nerdwallet.com/article/small-business/business-plan

Oakley, D. (2018, February 10). *What Are The Key Resources Needed To Deliver The Value Proposition?* Denis Oakley & Co. https://www.denis-oakley.com/key-resources/

Sample Funding Request and Return Statement. (2018, March 9). SME Toolkit Caribbean. https://republicsmetoolkit.com/sample-funding-request-and-return-statement/

Seven Common Business Plan Mistakes. (n.d.). https://web.uri.edu/risbdc/seven-common-business-plan-mistakes/

Software, P. A. (n.d.). *Financial Planning Business Plan - Financial Plan.*

References

Bplans: Business Planning Resources and Free Business Plan Samples. https://www.bplans.com/financial-planning-business-plan/financial-plan/

Sweeney, D. (2021, July 13). *Why Written Agreements Matter in Business.* The Story Exchange. https://thestoryexchange.org/why-written-agreements-matter-in-business-partnerships/?gclid=EAIaIQobChMI183224e4_AIVyBwrCh0hggDvEAAYAyAAEgKofPD_BwE

U.S Small Business Administration. (2019). *Write your business plan.* SBA. https://www.sba.gov/business-guide/plan-your-business/write-your-business-plan

Made in United States
North Haven, CT
17 August 2023

40428768R00109